SPOKANE, 22ND STREET AND THE FIFTIES

Marilyn Magney Newkirk

RAYMOND AND SCHAFER PUBLISHING

*Front Cover Photo: This is a picture of the Magney family taken in front of the fireplace
at Ben and Ruby Schafer's home on Seventeenth Avenue in Spokane, Washington.
The picture was taken in 1954.
Featured in the picture left to right in the back row are; Dorothy Magney, Jack Magney,
middle row, Janice Magney, front row, Marilyn Magney and Richard Magney.*

Published by
Raymond and Schafer Publishing
15343 – 105TH AVE SE
Yelm, WA. 98597
(360) 400-1756
rbn@comcast.net

ISBN-13: 978-1-886081-04-2
ISBN-10: 1-886081-04-2

Library of Congress Number: 2005927569

ACKNOWLEDGEMENTS

It is with deep gratitude that I acknowledge the many individuals who made it possible for me to write the stories of men and women who lived in Spokane Washington and made the small unknown town grow and flourish following World War II.

This book could not have been written without the assistance and patient support of my wonderful husband, Ray and our kids.

My daughter, Jeannette Hansen, made numerous phone calls on my behalf and collected pertinent information that was needed to complete different stories.

Janice Lewis, my sister, assisted me with finding, selecting, printing and arrangement of the many pictures used in the book.

Greg Newkirk has been my computer expert and assisted with taking the manuscript and making it disk ready for printing.

Son-in-law Mike Anderson, volunteered his time to assist with editing the manuscript.

My aunt and uncle, Jesse and Virginia Groff, my brother Richard Magney, along with long time friend Jane McKillip (Winton) and Shirley Newman (Nix), and her husband, Ken, contributed vast amounts of historical information and spent time selecting photographs and editing my mistakes.

Patty Collins (Eugene) and her mother Joan, along with Delores Allers and Irene Zilgme, greatly assisted me with writing the memories of life on 22nd street.

The story about the Crescent could not have been written without the help of two fine gentlemen, Mr. Jonathan Bixby and Mr. Cal Browne.

Linda Casimir, the Assistant Development Director at Northwest Christian School, went out of her way to supply me with vast amounts of history about the school and its beginning.

The staff of the Northwest Historical section of Spokane's downtown library offered untold help in searching through newspaper articles to confirm dates and names regarding early history about Spokane.

Beverly Woody, Joy Morgan, Becky Moonitz, and Loretta Borowski supplied other information and assistance.

My good friend, Betty Zachow, offered encouragement, faith, and spent hours editing my work. She never doubted my ability to write a story about the grassroots citizens of Spokane who made a positive impact on my life in the fifties.

A number of authors assisted with reference material from their books which aided me greatly in writing my story. They are: William Stimson, *A View of the Falls* published in 1999, Priscilla Gilkey, Margaret Crabtree, and Terren Roloff, *The Deaconess Story* published in 1996, Tony Bamonte and Suzanne Schaeffer Bamonte, *Manito Park A Reflection of Spokane's Past* published in 1998, Russell F. Weigley, *History of the United States Army* published in 1967, Leon H. Canfield, Howard B. Wilder, *The Making of Modern America* published in 1960, *The Spokesman-Review*, *Spokane Woman* and the Eastern Washington State Historical Society.

Spokane, 22nd Street And The Fifties

INTRODUCTION

Spokane, Twenty Second Street, And The Fifties is the story of my memories about Spokane and a number of its common citizens who were part of my life during the 1950s.

Some of the individuals were family members while others were neighbors and friends whose lives had a profound impact on my life. Many of these individuals played a vital role in the development and economics of Spokane. The remarkable individuals whom I talk about were not necessarily civic leaders or well known politicians or relatives to the founding fathers of Spokane Falls. Nevertheless, many of them played vital roles in what is Washington State's second largest city.

The story of *Spokane, 22nd Street, And The Fifties*, has elements of historical information about the city and its original growth up to the end of the 50s. The main purpose of this book is not to focus on the past history and the city fathers but instead, to intertwine this information with my life, my memories and memories of family and friends.

As a youngster I was raised on an unusual street on the South Side of Spokane. It was nestled in between two large and well known city parks. The closest to my home was Manito Park with its beautiful gardens and play areas. The other was Comstock Park with its Olympic size swimming pool where I spent many hot summer days either relaxing in the refreshing waters or learning how to swim.

First Presbyterian Church, Roosevelt Elementary School and Northwest Christian Grade School afforded me the opportunity to grow spiritually and intellectually. Neighbors like the Allers family, the Eugene family and the Zilgme family, along with Eric Bax van Werald, Erna Bert Nelson, and the Groff, Winton and Nix families helped to spur on interest and develop talents.

It is with a sense of gratitude and love for the city of Spokane that I share my memories. My ultimate hope is that in the course of spinning my stories, others might acquire knowledge as to what it was like to grow up in a mid-size town following World War II. My other purpose is to inform younger generations about another era. The glory days of the 50s, I believe, were filled with hope, excitement, creativity, innovative fashions and hair styles, new technology, the beginning of rock and roll music, and dynamic business prosperity and growth.

DEDICATION

Today is January 3, 2003. Ray and I are sitting on a large cluster of granite boulders stretched along the beach in Bichino, Tasmania. Years of salt water have smoothed the rocks to perfection. We are enjoying the warm sun rays and breathing clean fresh unpolluted air.

The beach is peaceful in this exotic, yet tranquil part of the world. The sun is warm, the breeze is light, and the temperature in the ocean water as it washes lightly over my feet is possibly 70 degrees. There are fewer than 20 other people on the beach. Several small fishing boats are anchored only a couple of hundred feet from the shore. All appear to be empty.

I feel as if I have been transported back in time as I sit peacefully looking at the clear blue sky that matches the color of the ocean. It's been a long time in coming; solitude, fresh air, peace and quiet, and Ray.

As we bask in this unbelievable setting, my mind reflects over the past six weeks.

December 3, I was called to the bedside of my mother, Dorothy Jean Magney, who at 85 was dying of Alzheimer's disease in a nursing home in Spokane.

Ray and I had been in Tennessee, to spend Thanksgiving with my youngest daughter, Teresa, her husband Michael, and my oldest granddaughter, Tianna. A second baby was due any moment, and we, of course, were hoping he or she would arrive before we had to return to the Northwest.

Thanksgiving week went by quickly. I cooked dinner for twelve of their military friends. Ray entertained Tianna with tickle wars and stories. Teresa grew larger and became more uncomfortable with each passing day.

On December 2, the baby had not yet arrived. With tears in our eyes, and lots of hugs and kisses we boarded the aircraft for our trip back to Seattle.

We arrived at Seattle International Airport (SEATAC) just before midnight, tired and anxious to get home. By 1:30 we had unpacked a few things and tumbled into bed, still bemoaning the disappointment at not being able to meet our newest grandchild.

I awoke about 8 a.m. and with a deep sense of urgency, and called my brother in Spokane. "You'd better come at once, Sis," he said, "Mom is dying. She hasn't taken food in days and she's waiting to see you." I told him we were on our way and with luck would arrive about 2:30 that afternoon. My last words to him were a plea to tell Mom to wait. I was on my way to her.

We did arrive about 2:30, a trip that seemed to me to take an eternity. As we pulled into the nursing home drive way, I jumped out and ran into the lobby, and down the hallway to her room. I remember praying, "Please, God, let Mom live long enough so I can kiss her one more time and tell her I love her before you take her home."

He granted my wish. As I entered her room, I could see that she was surrounded by her entire family – Virginia, her younger sister; Virginia's daughter Karen; my younger sister Janice; my daughter Jeannette, and her five year old daughter Samantha. My younger brother Richard, and Uncle Jess were near the doorway.

Janice put her arms around me and said, "We were praying you would get here in time."

I bent over my Mother and cupped her face in my hands. Gently, I said, "Mom. It's Marilyn. I am here. Thank you for waiting for me to get here so I could tell you how much I love you."

She was unconscious, I knew. But as I said those words, I could see her eyelids flutter and move. And along with that movement appeared a tear that began to trickle down the side of her face on her flawless skin. I knew, as did everyone in the room, that Mom realized I was there, and I would be with her on her final journey.

Our loving Lord granted me still another extended wish. Janice, Jeannette, and I were with Mom for three hours. All of a sudden at 6:04 p.m. on December 3, a miraculous sound and occurrence took place. There was a swishing sound and a whirling of wind in the room, a change in Mom's appearance. We felt the presence of God's angels as this windy, swishing noise engulfed the room. At 85, Dorothy Jean Magney slipped into the arms of our Heavenly Father.

Twelve hours later, Teresa gave birth to a baby girl whom she named Alexa Dorothy. "The Circle of Life;" a moment of sadness and loss, and a time for rejoicing and celebration was sustaining our family.

In honor of my mother and father, Jack Magney who passed away in August 1973, I want to share with friends and family a legacy of their lives, and the lives of friends and family members who shared in a special and unique relationship that crossed language barriers and religious differences during the fifties.

This is a story of love and hope, of heartache and sorrow, of triumph and victory. It is a story of friendship. It is a story about Jesus.

One of my father's favorite hymns was "What a Friend We Have in Jesus," and this song is filled with wonderful words that truly exemplify the lives of the families who lived in Spokane.

What a friend we have in Jesus; a friend, who sticks by us through thick and thin, a friend who is closer than a brother or sister. *Spokane, 22nd Street, And The Fifties* is about friendships, the lives of Jack and Dorothy, their love for Christ, and how they raised their children.

Brunot Hall Girls School in 1915. Charles Magney purchased the school in 1917 and renamed the building the Burnot Hall apartments.

THE CITY: IT'S RIVER, ITS LANDSCAPE

It was the majestic river that first lured the city founders to the area that was once known as Spokane Falls.

In William Stimson's book, *Spokane A View of the Falls*, "before white man appeared on the scene, the river was the home to the Spokane Indians. The name SPOKANEE means "Children of the Sun," and refers to the three Spokane tribes. The upper tribe was located near Lake Coeur d'Alene, the middle tribe around what is now the city of Spokane, and the lower tribe camped at the mouth of the Spokane River."

The river provided a rich source of food to the Indians. There was an abundance of salmon from the Pacific Ocean that swam up the Columbia River and spawned each summer in the Spokane River.

The river which runs through the heart of downtown Spokane is blessed with an abundance of gigantic basalt boulders that cascaded down a steep three tiered embankment. During the early spring season when the snow packs in the Cascade, Selkirk and Rocky Mountains melted, overflowing streams of water sooner or later merged into the Spokane River. The over abundance of water from the mountain streams caused the river levels to rise, thus sending thundering gushes of water to rapidly flow down over these monstrous basalt boulders. Watching the raging river is spectacular as foaming water crashes through the rocky gorge causing a powerful water fall that is a breathtaking sight to behold.

White settlers started appearing in the area around 1870. These early settlers immediately were drawn to the river and fell in love with its magnificent water fall. With time, they learned how to harness the rivers power, to run sawmills and flour mills, and to eventually light the homes and offices in this young city.

The landscape of Spokane and Eastern Washington is most unique. Giant rock formations of basalt boulders cover a large portion of Washington State and parts of Idaho and Oregon. Remnants of basalt flows are visible as steep slopes, basalt walls, and rocky outcroppings.   During the early history of Spokane, the city was isolated from the rest of the world by several separate mountain ranges, the Cascades to the west, the Selkirks to the northeast, the Bitterroots, the Coeur d' Alenes, and the Rockies to the east. To the south is the canyon where the Snake River flows.

Spokane is surrounded by numerous lakes and rivers. Today, and in the fifties, these lakes and rivers provide families with outdoor activities such as swimming, camping, hiking, exploring, fishing, and hunting. The forest areas are thick with wildlife such as deer and elk. The land is rich in huckleberries and huckleberry picking is a popular activity for families. From this wild berry one can make jams, syrups, pies, candies and even candles.

The surrounding forest land is rich with tall ponderosa pine, white pine, tamarack, cedar and douglas fir trees.

South of Spokane, in the Palouse area, the rolling hills and rich soil provide fertile ground for farmers to grow wheat that feeds the entire world. North of Spokane, in the Greenbluff Hills, are wonderful orchards bursting with numerous varieties of fruit trees. To the west of Spokane by almost 90 miles is the mighty Columbia River and to the east the lead mines of the Coeur d' Alenes.

IT SHOULD HAVE BEEN 22ND AVENUE!

Everyone in the neighborhood knew that. Everyone knows it now, and everybody knew it 60 and 70 years ago. In Spokane traffic driving east or west is on an avenue. Those driving north or south are on streets. But to families and friends on Spokane's South Hill in the 40s, 50s, "avenue" sounded a bit pretentious.

To many of the families who lived on the south side, or South Hill as many referred to this location, they most assuredly referred to their east and west directional locations as an avenue. To this special neighborhood on the south side of Spokane near Manito Park, 22nd was too short a street to be considered an avenue. The street was short and narrow and dotted with vacant lots, oversized home lots, small homes, big homes, old homes and a few new homes. 22nd Street was not a place where the hoity-toity, wealthy and the famous lived. 22nd Street was a neighborhood filled with the elderly, the young, the returning war veteran and refugees. It was a street where one would hear a variety of foreign languages spoken. Kids played on the street and neighbors sat on their front steps and watched. It was a quiet street, a clean street, with big trees and flowers in virtually every yard.

JACK AND DOROTHY

Like all cities in America, the people of Spokane were experiencing a sense of joy and relief. Loved ones who had fought in WWII were returning to their families and the hometowns they had left.

For many, and perhaps it was hardest on young married couples, the time apart had been four years or longer. Reuniting was a time for new beginnings and hopefully never having to say good-bye again.

This was the case for Jack and Dorothy Magney. While Jack was attending college at the University of Washington, President Roosevelt was sending our war material to England and the US Navy was escorting convoys half way across the Atlantic. At that time, Jack was an ROTC cadet who intended to become a full time Active Duty officer in the Army upon completion of college.

December 7, 1941. Hawaii. Pearl Harbor. "The date that will live in infamy." It changed those plans for Jack Magney and Dorothy Jean Schafer.

Jack and Dorothy met at Westminster Fellowship at First Presbyterian Church in Spokane when they were each nineteen. Both of their families had attended this old, established church located in the heart and center of downtown Spokane on 4th and Cedar.

It was only natural that these two young adults should be attracted to each other. Both were strikingly good looking. Dorothy was a tall, slender beauty with light olive skin and huge green eyes that seemed never to stop smiling. Her beautiful dark brown hair and satin complexion made her a knock-out! She loved people, loved to sing, and loved her church. She was always a positive and up-beat fun-loving person.

Jack, at just a shade less than six feet, was considered tall, dark, and handsome. He graduated from high school when he was 16, had been captain of the football team, and had a passion for music. He also had a passion for his church and for Jesus.

Because Jack and Dorothy loved to sing and both had outstanding voices, they sang in the church choir. Jack frequently sang solos. His marvelous, deep, rich, bass voice would fill the sanctuary of that beautiful old church.

Jack's love of music began in early childhood. As a boy, he lived in Spokane's Browne's Addition. This was the section of town where the upper crust of Spokane society had once lived. It was here that many of the city's founders had built their mansions and established their homes.

The old Patsy Clark Mansion, built by world famous architect Kirkland Cutter, was next door to Jack's family home.

As a young boy, he had a paper route where he delivered The Spokesman-Review to the Patsy Clarks, DoctorGrieves, Doctor White, and the Patterson family-all names familiar in Spokane history. The money he earned from his paper route he saved so he could buy an 1885 pump organ.

He never received formal music lessons. His natural ear for hearing music, and his tenacious desire to teach himself how to play the organ, made learning fun and easy.

The first songs he learned were hymns that he had known from church. His mother, Emma Magney, gave him an old church hymnal that she had received as a young girl.

As he learned the old hymns, one by one, he would accompany himself and sing the familiar words. With maturity his voice deepened and the rich bass tones became more prominent. Upon graduation from high school, he entered Gonzaga University where he sang with the popular Gonzaga glee club.

Dorothy didn't play a musical instrument, but her father, Benjamin Harrison Schafer, was always playing the harmonica or a violin as she was growing up.

Ben was one of nine German children born of immigrant parents, Adam and Mary Schafer, who settled in the Ponderosa area of the Spokane Valley.

All nine children were taught to play at least one instrument. Some played the saxophone, some the accordion, some the piano; but for Ben it was the harmonica and the violin.

Dorothy always said that her father had enough musical talent for the entire family. Her talent was to accompany her father with singing and whistling, which she did beautifully, while he played either of his instruments.

For both Jack and Dorothy, music was a daily part of their early lives, and it remained so their entire lives.

Jack and Dorothy were both raised in homes where a foreign language was spoken. Jack's parents, Charles and Emma Magney, spoke fluent Swedish. Charles was born in Stockholm and was one of four children. He had an older brother and twin sisters. He was about six or seven when his parents came to America. His father changed their last name from Magnusson to Magney.

I am not at all certain about Charles Magney's educational background. His family migrated from the East Coast to the Midwest and eventually headed to the Pacific Northwest, where many Norwegian and Swedish families were settling in Seattle and Spokane. The mining, fishing, and lumbering industries were attracting these Scandinavian immigrants.

For a number of years, Charles and his older brother John, worked in the mines in Harrison, Idaho. Eventually the brothers were able to save enough money to purchase small amounts of property in that area. As Charles grew older, his life revolved around buying and selling property in Spokane, and predominantly in the Browne's Addition.

As his small empire grew, Charles Magney became better known as C. A. Magney. Throughout his building career he acquired a reputation as a tough, hard crusted business developer in the city. For a number of years he had lavish office space in the Paulsen building, which at that time was the tallest building east of the Cascade Mountains. With a serious depression threatening the economy and his new empire, Charlie Magney gave up his plush office space in the Paulsen Building. He relocated his business and took up permanent residence in one of the apartment buildings that he owned. By age 39, he still had not married. Charles, like Emma, was a devoted Christian and attended the Lutheran church in the Browne's Addition section of Spokane.

Emma was born in a little Swedish village in northern Michigan. Neither spoke a word of English until they were six or seven years of age.

Emma was a brilliant child and as she grew, her inquisitive desire to learn and explore grew with her. She obtained her teaching certificate at nineteen. She taught grade school and high school in Michigan for several years. It was a one-room schoolhouse for all the children, regardless of their ages. Undoubtedly, few, if any, recognized how fortunate they were to have a teacher so well versed in English and Swedish, as well as Latin. She had found Latin to be mentally stimulating while still in high school, and had become fluent in both the writing and reading.

As Emma neared the age of 27, she and another friend who was also a spinster school teacher decided if they were to ever marry, they would need to leave their Michigan communities and become adventurous. They took a leap of faith and moved west in hopes of finding the men of their dreams. Those men, of course, must be of Swedish and Lutheran decent. They must speak Swedish, and most of all, be rich.

Emma and her friend left Michigan when Emma was almost 28. They headed west to find teaching jobs in Spokane. Both had read newspaper accounts that Spokane was a growing community with rich single men. Spokane also was building knew schools and searching for qualified school teachers. When the two women arrived in Spokane, they found an apartment in Browne's Addition, attended a nearby Lutheran Church and were quickly hired by the Spokane School District.

It was at that this Lutheran church that Charles Magney and Emma Larson were introduced, and their courtship began.

It was only natural that Charles would have been attracted to Emma. She was a tall, strikingly beautiful Swedish woman with a flawless complexion, sandy blonde hair and green eyes. She was poised and eloquent in her speech, spoke fluent Swedish, was a schoolteacher, and a devout Lutheran!

The courtship was a short one. They were married on November 29, 1916, in their Lutheran Church. On September 11, 1917, Jack Arnold Magney was born at Deaconess, a modern Methodist hospital in downtown Spokane.

Jack was to have only two homes. Both were in Browne's Addition. Jack's first was the Berkley apartments which his father owned. When Jack was two, Charles and Emma moved to the Brunot Hall apartments on Pacific Avenue. C. A. Magney, of course, owned these buildings. Their apartment was on the first floor and contained 1500 square feet. The apartment complex occupied half a city block, and was surrounded by lush green grass, shrubbery, tall oak and maple trees on one side and Patsy Clark Mansion on the other side.

The Brunot Hall apartment building had once been an exclusive private girl's school, where the wealthy could send their daughters to receive the best education possible. This school had been an institution in Spokane for many years.

Brunot Hall was a successor to Mary's Hall, which was built by the Rev. Charles B. Crawford on the site once occupied by the residence of August Paulson, for whom the Paulson building was named. The school was constructed by Mr. and Mrs. James Lyon when Bishop and Mrs. Samuel H. Wells arrived in Spokane in 1893.

The Brunot Hall was named after Felix Brunot of Pittsburg who contributed large sums of money to the school.

Mrs. Wells acted as the school principal. There were about 40 boarding pupils who came from all over the northwest. The day scholars numbered nearly100 due to the popularity of the school. The first graduate received her diploma from the school in 1893. Graduates from Brunot Hall continued on with their education and entered exclusive eastern colleges for girls.

In his will, Felix Brunot left $33,000, to be invested in the girl's school. Within a few years, however, the school was plagued with numerous problems. There was a movement in the Pacific Northwest for better high schools. Spokane was a great promoter of this concept. According to an article in The Spokesman-Review regarding the status of Brunot Hall in 1917, "the school showed the effects of the diminished attendance of both boarding and the day scholars." At the same time this was happening, the rentals in the Felix Building which was located on First and Madison were showing a decline. It was revenues from these rentals that helped to support the school. To stem the financial problems resulting from the decline in students and lower revenues, the school was sold in 1917.

On Saturday, August 18, 1917, The Spokesman- Review ran an article about the school. This story came as a surprise to many people. The newspaper article states, "The school is to be divided into the junior and senior high school. Students will be prepared for college in 11 years. The primary department will include the lower four grades, while the high school course will have seven years work."

The school continued to struggle financially, and in 1919, C. A. Magney purchased the school and converted this elite girls' school into an apartment building.

The building itself had three floors and a basement area that housed the boiler, maintenance and storage areas. The basement level of the building was so large that C.A. Magney was able to build four good sized studio apartments. The most striking interior features were the breathtakingly wide stairway with solid wood mahogany railing, and the plush oriental carpet that graced the inside of the staircase.

On the huge walls in the common area were old oil paintings that were mounted with wide heavy ornate baroque gold frames. Pictures ranged in size upward from 14 x20 to 30 x 40. Most of the pictures were themes from the old country. Italian tapestries could also be seen in the halls and one, in fact, was on the wall in the Magney apartment. In front of the tapestry sat a long ornate desk where Emma paid bills, greeted and interviewed new tenants and received monthly rental checks.

Dorothy Jean Schafer's life style was completely the opposite of Jack's. She was born at Deaconess Hospital in

Spokane on July 11, 1917. She was raised on the north side of the Spokane River, the dividing point between the two sides of Spokane.

Dorothy's parents, Ben and Ruby Schafer, rented a number of homes on the north side. This was the part of town where the average middle class worker lived and raised his family. As Dorothy was growing up, her parents moved often and she lived in five different houses. Ben and Ruby always rented, and never owned their own home until 1939, when they purchased the two story house on 17th near Manito Park on the south side of the river.

Ben and Ruby were devoted Christians. They lived a life style that was totally opposite from Charles and Emma Magney. Their lives were more of a humble and frugal existence. Ben was a dairyman, and to supplement their income, he and Ruby also ran a small eating stand where Ruby did all the cooking.

There were many differences, but the common thread between the two families was that both Emma and Ruby were born in Michigan about the same time. Ruby's family moved to the Pacific Northwest when she was about nine. Her family homesteaded thirty miles north of Spokane near Clayton and Deer Park. Ruby's parents settled in that location so her father, Chauncey Doyen, could work in the lumber mills at Deer Park, and raise horses to sell to the Colville Indians.

Ruby's mother, Mary Anne Chamberlain Doyen, raised four daughters. She was a wonderful cook and helped Chauncey work their farm. She was a devout Methodist woman who took deep pride in her faith and saw to it that the Sabbath was honored at their little country home. This meant she and Chauncey, together with their four daughters, would spend the greatest part of each Sunday at church.

Ruby looked like her father, as she had his bright, thick, auburn hair. She inherited her mother's round face, rosy complexion and bright green eyes.

She was close to her parents and sisters and soon developed a talent for cooking, sewing, and decorating. She loved to knit and crochet. Formal education was not stressed in her home, and she was never exposed to a foreign language. Her talent, because this was the mark of a good girl, was in the making of her own clothing and developing the ability to take a nickel and make it look like a dollar.

Ruby, her sisters and the women from the country Methodist church would get together and have regular quilting bees. She took great pride in the fact that her home was always immaculate; when someone said one could eat off her floor the statement was literally true.

Ben's parents, Adam and Mary Schafer, migrated to the Pacific Northwest and pioneered the Ponderosa area of the Spokane Valley. Ben Schafer's parents had both been orphans who came to America when they were in their late teens. They were farmers, and made an income from selling water from the Schafer's Mineral Springs. Ben was the sixth of nine children.

Education was not necessarily a priority in this poor German family. Around 1897, Ben began school, in the little town of Chester, Washington. At the age of nine, he did not know a single word of English.

While there may have been a lack of education and material things, God blessed this sweet German family with the ability to laugh and face life with a positive attitude. Come Sunday, the family loaded into the buggy and headed for church. Adam was sometimes asked to deliver the sermon. He was a devoted Baptist who taught his children how to pray, and the importance of having a relationship with God.

Ben and Ruby met at Liberty Lake one summer. Their courtship continued for a number of months as they attended church functions and social gatherings at Liberty Lake, where one of Ben's older sisters, Sophia, had a home on the lake.

Liberty Lake is located in the Spokane Valley, near the Idaho, Washington border, and was almost ten miles east of the Schafer homestead. Liberty Lake back in 1912 -1920 was about a thirty minute ride on the street car or train to the Idaho state line.

According to all the Schafer clan and especially my mother, Liberty Lake was one of Spokane's first resort areas and regularly hosted lavish affairs. In fact, Grandpa used to recall that in the early 1900's, several thousand folks could be seen in their finest attire promenading along the sandy beaches, swimming or renting rowboats or just meandering around the lake on a Sunday afternoon. It was one of the places Grandpa Schafer enjoyed most in his youth and courting years. The lake afforded people the opportunity to get away from the drudgeries of life, the hard work of farming and provided time for fun, relaxation and merriment.

Historical documents in The Spokesman-Review show that the lake was discovered in 1871 by a young man named Steve Liberty. Those stories report that he acquired a 160 acre homestead on what became known as the Wicomico Beach. Liberty was later joined by his friend, Joe Peavy, Spokane's first blacksmith. Peavy homesteaded on the northeast side of the lake. In

1900, a wealthy Montanan named Charlie Traeger built a lodge at the lake. Charlie named the lodge the Zepher Hotel and Casino. The Zepher featured an outdoor dance pavilion adjacent to a sumptuously furnished two-story, 20 room mansion.

I remember hearing Grandpa sharing stories with his brothers and sisters about the all-night dances, the lavish Thanksgiving, Christmas and New Year's Eve affairs that were held at the Zepher. As I learned later in life, those all-night dance parties were very scandalous in the eyes of great Grandma and Grandpa Schafer. So it was with great care that the party information did not get back to them.

Farmers would travel by horse and buggy, while others would board the electric trains that departed from Spokane's Inland Empire depot for Liberty Lake. This ride usually took about forty-five minutes. Grandpa and Grandma Schafer would often say that the best time for a gathering was on a Saturday night, when they would congregate around a big bonfire built along the shore. There they would roast hot dogs and sausages, and drink piping hot coffee.

By 1910, Liberty Lake had six resorts that flourished on the lake. The Wayside Resort offered cabins, Ted Week's had rides for kids, and Sandy Beach boasted a dance slab. According to Grandma, it was great fun to watch people dancing. This was a practice that was greatly frowned on by her Methodist mother and grandpa's Baptist father.

Another one of the highlights for Ben and Ruby during their courtship was to attend the popular Natatorium Amusement Park, which was situated on the Spokane River.

A favorite ride at the park was the grand old antique carousel that played the Straus waltzes. It was during one of these rides that Ben proposed to Ruby.

Dorothy Jean was not their first child. Ben and Ruby were married a year and a half when Ruby gave birth to a little boy who was named Raymond. At two months of age, Raymond became seriously ill with pneumonia. With nothing in those days to offset this dreadful disease, it claimed Raymond's life. Less than two years following Raymond's death, Ruby gave birth to a little girl and named her Dorothy Jean. She was to become the apple of her father's eye, and could do nothing wrong. Dorothy was my mother. In time, two other babies joined the family—Virginia and Donald.

Dorothy attended North Central High School and was active in school affairs. She was not, however, particularly interested in academics, and would have preferred the title of "Party Queen" had such a title been offered. She loved to have fun and socialize.

Classmates gravitated toward her enthusiasm for life. Many remained friends through all the long years of her life. When Dorothy died at age 85, scores of her grade school and high school friends were still in touch with her.

Following graduation, Dorothy worked for a florist. She later worked for Dr. Elizabeth White and then Dr. Irene Grieve, both prominent ob/gyn physicians in Spokane.

Jack proposed to Dorothy shortly after August 31, 1940, when a presidential order activated his unit, the 161st Infantry Regiment. His reporting date for one year of active duty was September 16, 1940.

Like any other young girl, Dorothy had dreams of a big church wedding; wearing the traditional long white wedding gown, seeing the church altar banked in an array of beautiful white and pink roses, the bridal party gowned and dressed to match the beautiful flowers. Now with the realization that America was preparing to fight against the Germans in Europe, and the daily pressure from the Japanese in the Pacific, their peaceful lives had been turned upside down.

Like many young couples who were in similar situations, they decided to be married in a small quiet ceremony at the home of Dorothy's parents. Their favorite pastor from First Presbyterian, Dr. Calhoun, officiated at the ceremony where their family and a few close friends gathered. Dorothy wore a simple mauve suit, Jack wore his uniform.

Little did they or their loved ones realize that they would soon be separated for four long years. Jack was sent to the South Pacific, where he spent most of that time as a second Lieutenant. Dorothy also believed it was her duty to serve her country in some capacity. She left her job with Dr. White and began work as a secretary in the accounting department at the Air Depot, now known as Fairchild Air Force Base in Spokane.

Schafer Road in Spokane Valley was named after great grandfather Adam Schafer and his oldest son Will Schafer.

A brief summary of Jack's military career:

The 161st Rifle Regiment was activated on September 16, 1940 as part of the 41st Infantry Division. The 161st assembled and trained at Fort Lewis, Washington. Exercises were held under the watchful eyes of Lt. Colonel Mark Clark and Colonel Dwight D. Eisenhower. The regiment's one year active duty was extended. Early in November, 1941, the 161st was cut out of the 41st Division and ordered to the Philippines.

The night before the Japanese attacked Pearl Harbor, the Regiment left for San Francisco. The news of the attack was received more with disbelief than shock as the report of the raid was orally passed to the men on the trains going south. The move to the Philippines was canceled, and the Regiment took up guard positions in the San Francisco area. Then in mid-December, 1941, the Regiment sailed for Hawaii on the Lurline, Matsonia, Monterey and the Bliss.

Some of the men landed Christmas Eve with smoke still rising from the Pearl Harbor attack December 7th. In Hawaii, the 161st performed guard duty for various military installations on Oahu. During October 1942 the regiment had joined the 25th Infantry Division and became the 161st Regimental Combat Team with the addition of the 89th Field Artillery Battalion and Company A, 65th Engineers.

The Regiment Commander was Colonel Clarence Orndorff from Spokane. In later years, Dad would work for Colonel Orndorff in Spokane. Ironically, when Col. Orndorff retired from the military, he started a thriving law practice, and years later my uncle, Jim Winton joined the firm and became a partner.

Almost a year later, the 161st, fought in Guadalcanal. The action there by the 161st was so fast and decisive that the 25th Division, which until this time was without a shoulder patch, was given a Taro Leaf, familiar to the Hawaiian Islands, with a bolt of lightning running through it. The morale of the 161st increased with the issuing of this insignia.

The Guadalcanal story had started four months before the 161st arrived. The area had been occupied by one Army division plus some Marines, but the effort had reached a stalemate. The 161st, as part of the 25th, was to turn the tide.

The attitude of the 161st was apprehension, in the eyes of their regular army sister Regiments. They took over defensive positions of the Marines on the Mataikau River. The division was picked to spearhead the first major attack against the enemy in months. The movement of the 161st was so rapid and decisive, it was left with this mission for the rest of the campaign, which lasted until they linked up with the 2nd Battalion, 132nd Infantry at Cape Esperance on February 9, 1943.

In 19 days of combat, the unit had covered 20 miles of beach and enemy infested jungle. At the end of the campaign, the Division Commander, General Collins, told the Regiment they were no longer a question mark in the eyes of their sister Regiments.

On February 7th, Col. Clarence A. Orndorff was ordered to the states because of illness, and Col. James L. Salton assumed command. On July 17th, 1943 the Regiment embarked for New Georgia, and was assigned to the 37th Infantry Division from Ohio. The first major action for the 161st was on Hastings Ridge and Tank Hill. Intense fighting took place for 5 days, and for 6 days more they defended their gains against counter attack. Hastings Ridge was named for 1st Lieutenant Charles J. Hastings from Walla Walla, Washington, who died there. After Hastings Ridge, the 161st fought to the beach via the Zieta Trail, and this ended the main phase of the battle for New Georgia. The Munda air strip was secured August 7, 1943. The Regiment was sent to New Zealand for a period of rebuilding depleted ranks and supplies. They remained there from November 15, 1943, until February 24, 1944, when they were sent to New Calondonia for further training.

On January, 11th, 1945, the Regiment, with the rest of the 25th Division, clambered down rope nets, poured into landing craft, and started for the beaches of an island known as Luzon in the Philippine Islands. They landed in San Fabian area on the west shore of the island, and drove across the central plain of Luzon. They crashed into the enemy six days later at Binalonan.

On the 26th of January, they smashed through San Manul. It was here that the last 13 officers of the original 114 officers who were inducted with the 161[st,] experienced an unofficial reunion and called themselves the dirty dozen. After that came Bryan Hill, Dig Dig, Dunken and Dalton Pass. Dalton Pass was the new name given to Balete Pass, where one of the toughest battles of the Pacific took place. Its fall was the key to the Luzon campaign. The Luzon Campaign lasted 165 days. The 161st had been in combat 225 days, a record equaled by few Regiments in the war.

War came to an end in Europe in the spring of 1945. Japan surrendered in August of 1945. The 161st marched ashore in the Wakayma area in Japan on October 2, 1945. After a short period, the 161st was relieved from assignment to the 25th Division and on November 1, 1945 the Regiment was deactivated at Nagoya, Japan. Lt. Colonel Bankston returned the colors to the State of Washington.

On June 17, 1946, the 161st Infantry was reassigned to the 41st Division. Activation of the Regiment started on March 24, 1947, with the Regimental Headquarters in Spokane, Washington.

In 1957, the Pentomac concept was proposed, the Division would go from three Regiments to five Battle Groups. In 1959, the 161st was re-designated as the 1st and 2nd Battle Groups of the 161st. Col. Ralph Phelps was made the Commander of the 1st of the 161st.

In the early 1950s Lt. Jack Magney was promoted to Captain, and worked directly for Col Ralph Phelps for the remainder of his military career.

During the 1950s, the Washington Infantry was greatly concerned with civil defense activities. The Cold War with Russia was looming over the country, and the military was very concerned with the possibility of facing a nuclear attack from Russia. Many of the personnel of the 161st had classified missions. They had two important concerns. The first was creating evacuation routes and assisting with evacuation drills, and the other was to encourage the citizens to be actively prepared by building bomb shelters in their own homes.

In 1946, Jack Magney went to work for the Washington National Guard.

Picture of First Presbyterian Church
showing the new Sunday School building on the left of the picture.

GRANDPARENTS
THE MAGNEYS AND THE SCHAFERS

The Magneys

How fortunate I was to be blessed with two sets of grandparents when I was growing up. More important was the fact that they lived in the same city, and were virtually only five minutes apart.

The C.A. Magneys lived at the Brunot Hall Apartments up to the end of their very elderly years. As a child, I loved to go with Dad to visit Grandma and Grandpa Magney. Sometimes this would be on a Saturday morning, so we could give Mom some time to herself, and at other times, this would be on a Tuesday or Wednesday evening. While Dad would visit with his parents, I would wonder around the inside of the apartment building, and pretend it was my own castle or mansion with it's long, wide staircases that resembled something out of a southern mansion such as the Tara mansion in *Gone With the Wind*. The carpet in the long, wide hallways and on the staircase was a thick, heavy fabric with a profound ornate design in it. I often thought it would have been great fun to try sliding down that elegant stair banister. But the thoughts of my father catching me and feeling the stinging pain from his belt was the only deterrent that was needed to confirm my thought that it would be an unwise decision.

In Grandma and Grandpa's apartment, the furnishings were old and simple, with dark furniture that had an Italian or French look and feel. I don't think Grandma had purchased a new sofa or chair since my father was born. The apartment was always neat and orderly. According to Grandma, this was very important because her living room was also the office where she conducted business with her tenants and various vendors. Even the top of her business desk was immaculate.

As a child, I was always fascinated with the large Queen Anne cherry wood desk that sat at the front of the apartment. By the side of the desk sat a huge wing back chair for the tenants to sit in while they were paying their bills or sharing their concerns with Grandma. It was at this desk that I learned to print my first letters and make the $ sign. According to Grandma Magney, this would be the most important sign I would ever make in my life time. It was, therefore, most important that I develop a great understanding of what the dollar sign stood for, and why it would always be so important in my life. I was six years old and starting the first grade when she taught me how to make that dollar sign $. The learning opportunity took place one hot summer Saturday afternoon, while Dad and Grandpa were fixing some plumbing and electrical problems in the building. For about an hour, I had Grandma's full attention. She made small dollar signs and large dollar signs. She would put the pencil in my hands and gently guide my small fingers with her larger Scandinavian hands, so together we could trace this important sign. Of course, at that time in my life I didn't realize the significance or the importance of that special sign. As a former school teacher, Grandma Magney also believed it was most crucial for me to know the letters in my first name, and how to spell my name. Grandma was rather upset to think that my mother had not prepared me for first grade by teaching me the importance of holding a pencil, the alphabet and how to spell *Marilyn*. We spent another hour playing school. It is a memory that will always live within my heart. Grandma Magney got to relive her former years as a school teacher, and I got to benefit from her great desire and gift of teaching.

The memories that I have of Grandma Magney are more sad than happy. I never really remember her smiling or laughing. She was always very serious with her conversations and had very few friends. Even though her dream of marrying a rich Swedish man had come to pass, I know her marriage to my grandfather was neither a happy or fulfilled marriage. Grandpa was a developer, builder, and a gambler. For every dollar he made he probably lost two. Emma had to be very industrious with her business apptitude to recuperate the losses, and multiply many times over what income she could. Because of Grandpa's gambling, over the years she became very sullen, withdrawn and focused solely on the business of managing the Brunot Hall Apartments and taking care of her two children.

Emma Magney was a very proper lady and was very proud of the fact that she was a business woman and a former school teacher. She always had the air and appearance of a woman of education, and "good breeding", and admitted to the fact that she enjoyed the intellectual company of men to women. She preferred the discussions of current events, politics and finances to conversation in who was getting married and who had the most money. Emma preferred to be known as Mrs. C. A. Magney. As a child, I never heard anyone call her by her given name of Emma. This was very sad, as I loved the name Emma, and thought it had a wonderful old-fashioned quality to it.

Grandma always dressed the part of a business woman, wearing lovely, expensive, silk dresses that were purchased in the dress salon of the Crescent department store where the wealthy and the social elite of Spokane purchased their expensive or stylish wearing apparel. Emma was not impressed with those who were part of the social elite of Spokane's society, but Grandpa was. She had the money to wear nice and rather expensive clothing and jewelry, and believed it was important for her to look professional at all times. Therefore, the ends justified the means. Even though Emma wore lovely clothing and fine conservative jewelry, she never wore make up. I am not sure why she chose not to wear cosmetics, nor did it make much difference, because her skin was almost flawless, even in her later years of life. The lack of make up went with her sullen look.

I never once saw Grandma Magney wearing a housecoat, which was a simple dress that most women wore in the 30s, 40s, and 50s. This garment would be worn in the house while performing house cleaning chores such as mopping the floors, running the vacuum, ironing the clothes, etc. As the late 50s approached, and pants and suits for women became very popular, Emma was appalled that women would consider wearing such sinful and disgusting looking garments.

According to Grandma, a woman who put on a pair of pants was definitely "lower class with no proper up bringing." Another appalling event for Grandma was to see a woman smoke a cigarette. This was a favorite topic of conversation for her. She was adamant in her conviction that women who smoked were uneducated, from lower class families, and definitely did not know the Lord or attend church.

Emma loved to travel, but most of her traveling she did without Grandpa. I am not sure why Grandma and Grandpa Magney took separate vacations. Maybe it was her way of escaping, for a few weeks out of the year, the responsibilities of managing a business. It was possibly giving herself a retreat away from Grandpa. Her travels usually took her back to Michigan to see her relatives or to Europe. She loved Europe. When I was young, she tried to make a trip once a year to visit the Scandinavian countries, Germany or Switzerland. She seemed to take great pleasure in the annual summer vacation that Grandpa insisted we take as a family. These summer excursions took us to California or to Canada.

Grandma had a housekeeper who came every day to tidy up the apartment, take care of the laundry, and fix lunch for her and Grandpa. I never saw my Grandma dust a piece of furniture, push a vacuum, wash or iron the clothes, or make a bed. She was too busy managing the apartment business and handling the finances.

Grandpa Magney's personality was quite the opposite of Grandma Magney's.

Grandpa's office was in the basement of the apartment building. This office was crammed with book cases that circled his entire office. The book cases were filled with many old books that were written in Swedish and had been owned by his father. There were law books, architectural books, books about the history of Washington and Idaho. Grandpa's office reminded me of a private library that was filled with books on every subject from all over the world. On one wall in Grandpa's office sat a very large solid oak roll top desk that was always pilled high with papers. One of the most fascinating features about his old desk was all of the little drawers and slots it contained. I am sure it had enough space for a zillion envelopes and a hundred rolls of stamps from all over the world. In front of Grandpa's desk was a rich leather executive chair fit for a prosperous businessman. Grandpa's office was always messy and cluttered, but to a child, it was a place where one could spend hours looking at all the books and admiring all the pictures that hung on the wall. High above the book cases hung huge ornate paintings that were framed in gold baroque.

Charles Magney was a rather flamboyant person. He enjoyed hobnobbing with those of wealth and position in Spokane. In his younger years before the stock market crash, his offices in the Paulsen building were furnished with rich red velvet drapes, heavy ornate furniture and oil paintings imported from Europe.

As a child, it was always fun to visit Grandpa Magney because he liked to give us money. In fact, Grandpa liked to draw attention to himself by flaunting money around his friends and family. C.A. enjoyed eating at the fanciest restaurants, staying at the most elaborate hotels and having a mob of people surrounding him. Grandpa always wanted to be recognized by the public.

In the summer months he always insisted on taking the family on a two week vacation. Sometimes this meant taking the other set of grandparents, along with all of his kids and grandkids. At times, I think he did this to draw attention to himself. Wherever we went, C.A. Magney made sure we stayed at the fanciest, or the ritziest, hotel in town.

His weakness in life was cards. He could not resist poker games, especially if the stakes were high. In his younger years, he was fairly sharp with the cards. As the years slipped by, his eye sight deteriorated, his hearing faded, and his mental sharpness declined, C.A. Magney lost a lot of money at the gambling tables.

I do not remember Grandpa Magney being loving, gentle or tender towards Grandma Magney. Much of the time, they conversed in Swedish. I did not see him hold her hand, kiss her lips or lovingly touch her.

Life seemed to always revolve around who he was, what he wanted and how he wanted to be recognized. Even at church, it was important for him to be seated in a certain section of the sanctuary so the senior pastor could recognize that C.A. Magney was present.

Grandma and Grandpa Magney lived in a section of Spokane referred to as Browne's Addition, which is one of the oldest developments in Spokane.

Browne's Addition was platted during the early 1880's. James Glover, considered the "father of Spokane," named the streets after the indigenous trees-Cedar, Walnut, Maple, Ash, Elm, Pine, Chestnut, Hemlock, Spruce, and Poplar.

Famous landmarks in Browne's Addition are Gus Sanders, Boston Meat Market, which served customers for more than 50 years, and the Elk Drug Store, which sat on Pacific for many years.

Within the Browne's Addition area is the Coeur d'Alene Park, the first and oldest park in Spokane. It is locate along Second Avenue, between Chestnut and Spruce Streets.

One of the first churches in the Browne's Addition area (and in Spokane) was the Emmanuel Lutheran Church. It was started by the Rev. Carl A. Horn and the Rev. Henry Ricke, who were traveling missionaries spending part of their time in the Spokane Falls area. In 1886 and 1887, they began the formation of a Lutheran Church of German speaking people.

The Emmanuel Lutheran church was officially organized by Rev. Hein in 1889. The church was built in 1890 at Third and Cowley. The second church was built in 1910 at Fourth and Pine. In 1959, the present worship center which sits at South 314 Spruce was dedicated, with the completion of a new education center.

The Rev. Paul Groschupf served as pastor between 1894 and 1924, and was succeeded at his death by his son, Rev. John Groschupf, who served from 1925 until 1957.

Charles and Emma Magney became friends of both Rev. Paul and Rev. John.

In the early years of Spokane's history, the founding families such as the Cowles, the Whites and the Finches kept their milk cows in a common pasture, and traded vegetables over the fence.

In the days before dairy routes, Browne's Addition families got milk from their own cows, taken back and forth daily to pasture by a neighborhood herder.

Browne's Addition was named after J. Browne who came to the city of Spokane Falls in 1878. He acquired 160 acres of land, and according to historical documents became Spokane's first millionaire by 1890.

In the early years Browne's Addition had some of the most popular real estate in the Pacific Northwest. In 1900, the Browne's sold their mansion to the railroad giant, Robert Strahorn. The Browne's moved farther south and built a lavish home on the mountain near Moran Prairie. Later in Spokane's history, the mountain would be named after Mr. Browne. By then, the Indian teepees on the west side were no longer present, and in their place stood the mansions of Spokane's new elite. Many of these mansions displayed the eclectic genius of Spokane's distinguished architect, Kirkland K. Cutter.

One of Cutter's most brilliant houses had no financial restraints. Given a blank check by mining millionaire Patrick F. (Patsy) Clark, Cutter designed and constructed the Clark mansion at West 2208 Second Avenue. The specially formed circular exterior brick towers were made of Italian sepia and sandstone. Throughout the home were hand carved detailings, French ceiling paintings, gilt columns, Egyptian gopher wood, and hand woven Beauvais tapestry wall-coverings. Included in the mansion were a tiffany peacock stained-glass window and a grandfather clock which, brought the cost of Patsy's mansion to one million dollars in 1898.

As a child, I remember playing at the Clark mansion. On several different occasions my father took me to the house so I could meet the people who were living at this castle. When Daddy was growing up, he said that Grandpa and Mr. Clark had been good friends.

Daddy periodically mentioned that Grandpa had promised Mr. Clark that he would care for Mrs. Clark if she should outlive her husband. True to Grandpa Magney's word, Mrs. Clark came to live at the Brunot Hall apartments following the death of Patsy Clark.

As a child, I loved to look at the Clark mansion while sitting on the front steps of the mansion. To me it resembled a castle from one of the Disney movies like Cinderella. I would pretend it was my own mansion. I actually felt very comfortable inside the home, because the stair cases and the paintings with the heavy baroque frames resembled the pictures and the staircase that were inside the Brunot Hall apartment house. I was also fascinated by the stained glass windows. They reminded me of the immense stained glass windows that occupy the sanctuary of First Presbyterian Church. Oh, I so badly wished that I could have been born in another era.

Daddy shared with me that the Clark family was fairly large and the family made extensive use of the upstairs ballrooms. The Clarks were known for entertaining the socially and musically prominent in Spokane.

Between 1885 and 1915, Browne's Addition reached the heights of its glamour era. The homes were large, lavish, and stately. Beautiful old trees were seen every- where. One could hear the echo of horses' hooves as they pulled the wealthy of Spokane's founding families: the Browne's, Clarks, Campbell's, and White's.

As the era of the silk hat passed quietly on to the business of the twentieth century, Browne's Addition settled into an established upper class neighborhood. The automobile opened the winding streets of Spokane's steep South Hill to more elaborate and upscale mansions. With the construction in 1890 of Spokane's first apartment buildings, the Colonial at West 2020-2030 Elm, the Avenida and the Westminster, the area eventually became attractive to college students, young couples and the retired or widowed. Its clear physical boundaries gave it a distinct identity. Eventually, street cars and electric trains enhanced its convenience to down town business and outlying recreation spots such as Liberty Lake.

A SIDE NOTE.

According to an article written in the Eastern Washington State Historical Society, in the early history of Spokane, "Brownes Addition was a state of mind."

By 1958, a big transition had been made. A number of areas were rezoned R-3 and R-4 and multi family dwellings became popular.

Historical preservationists, realtors, and Browne's Addition residents are now actively working to preserve the once beautiful and elegant mansions that were the beginning of Spokane Falls, and eventually Spokane.

The Schafers

The joy of my life was being the granddaughter of Ben and Ruby Schafer. Grandma and Grandpa Schafer's home on 17th Avenue abounded with love, laughter and much happiness.

Grandma and Grandpa Schafer lived about six and half blocks from our home on 22nd Street. Best of all, they were only one block away from the wonderful duck pond at Manito Park, and only four and half blocks from my grade school, Roosevelt Elementary School.

How I adored and loved Grandma and Grandpa Schafer. The fondest memories of my childhood, youth and early adult years revolved around the moments I spent with these two remarkable individuals.

I loved going to their home, and took every opportunity to do so. Many times I would make arrangements with Grandma Schafer to come by for lunch. Lunch time at Roosevelt grade school was usually 45 minutes or an hour in length. Most of the time, I would ride my bicycle to school. It took me just a few minutes to get from school to their home on 17th Avenue. The minute that I would walk through the back door of their home, I would smell the aroma of freshly baked cookies, pies or cakes.

Ruby Schafer was known by friends and family to be one of the best cooks in Spokane. Her pies could not be beat. To this day, I have never had a pie crust that was as flaky and light as hers. Grandma's cakes were the tallest I have ever seen, and each type of frosting that she made would melt in one's mouth.

My favorite meal at the Schafer house was the home made chicken and noodle casserole dish. It was so much fun to watch Grandma make the dough from scratch for the noodles. She would take a large pottery bowl, a wooden spoon, dip into her flour drawer and scoop out four cups of flour and pour the flour into the pottery bowl. Next, she would add the eggs. I think she used one egg for every cup of flour. She would thoroughly mix the flour and the eggs, until the consistency was thick like pie dough. Then she would take the rolling pin and lay the noodle dough on her kitchen table, and roll out the dough so it resemble pie dough. Next she would cut wide strips of dough and let them dry for a day before she would drop the noodles into the rich flavorful chicken broth that was full of big chunks of tender chicken.

Grandpa Schafer said he didn't have a favorite meal but I noticed that he was always asking her to prepare sauerbraten and sauerkraut for him. Mom liked her mother's lamb stew, and other members of the family were always asking Grandma to make her fried chicken when we would have family gatherings.

One of the favorite times of the year for the family was fall. Grandpa was an avid sportsman. He loved to go hunting and fishing with all of his cronies. Come October and November, he was either hunting for duck or deer. Friends and family looked forward to receiving an invitation to Ruby's home for one of her duck dinners or her venison steak meals. Grandpa was very generous in sharing portions of the deer meat with his kids. Everyone received sausage and venison roast. This was like receiving a pre-holiday present from Ben and Ruby Schafer.

My grandmother was one of the most remarkable ladies whom I have ever known. She was a lady in the truest sense of the word. I had never heard her raise her voice to anyone. The words that flowed from her ruby red lips were always kind and gentle. Her theory was if you can't say something nice about someone then don't say anything. Grandma, however, had a way with words. Many times in order to get a point across, instill words of wisdom, or offer encouraging remarks, she would use one of many old fashioned phrases such as;

- "It's a long road that has no end."
- "Find a way or make one."
- "If wishes were horses, beggars could ride."
- "Tell the truth and shame the devil."
- "You are known by the company you keep."
- "Praise is like perfume; it is to be sniffed and enjoyed, but never swallowed."
- "Pretty is as pretty does."
- "The road to hell is paved with good intentions."
- "Do not judge a book by its cover."

Grandma was always prim and proper with her speech as well as her appearance. This was possibly due to the fact that her mother was very English.

Even though Ruby's mother was a farmer's wife, she believed that a lady must always look and act the part. Her home should be immaculate at all times; the food should be not only delicious but served on fine china with fine linens.

Ruby's day began at 5 am, sometimes even sooner. She was the first one into the bathroom. When she made her exit from the bathroom, she had bathed, dressed, styled her hair, and applied her make up to perfection. No one ever saw a hair out of place. She always looked like a sparkling rose and could have passed for a fashion model day or night. Even when she wore her house coat first thing in the morning, she looked like a fashion model. By 6:45 in the morning, she would have mopped at least one floor or started a load of wash, and was in the process of setting the table for breakfast. After washing the breakfast dishes, she would bake a batch of cookies or make one of her famous pies. Her goal was to be out of her house coat by 9:00 am, dressed in one of her pretty dresses, and ready to meet the world for the remainder of the day. After she was dressed and ready to meet the world, she set aside one half hour for her individual Bible study and devotional time. She always said that if she missed that time with Jesus, her day never went right.

Both Grandma and Grandpa Schafer were very involved at First Presbyterian Church. Grandma had been a Deaconess for years. Two days out of the week, she was off to the hospital or the nursing home to take flowers to church members or friends. The flowers that she took were grown by Grandpa either in his greenhouse or came directly from the yard. Along with flowers would always be a Bible verse and a prayer for the person. Ruby was also very involved with one of the women's circles and the ladies association at the church. One morning out of every week, she would gather with a group of ladies to pray for members of the church.

Ben was as much involved with First Presbyterian Church as Ruby. For many years he served as a greeter and an usher, and periodically was a Deacon. Ben was known for more than growing gorgeous roses and begonias. He had a remarkable sense of humor and never met a stranger. He had a unique gift for making everyone feeling welcomed and appreciated, whether it was in his home or at church. Grandpa had two different styles for greeting people. His hand was always out first, and the grip in his hand was strong and firm. While he was shaking a man's hand, he had his other hand firmly on the man's

Ben and Ruby Schafer sitting in front of the fireplace at their home on 17th. (1954)

shoulder saying, "Gosh, it is so good to see you, may God richly bless this day for you." For the ladies, his greeting was very different. He loved to make the ladies feel good about themselves. He had the wonderful hand shake for them but instead would say, "My! You are the prettiest lady I have seen today, God bless you, dear."

According to Mom, when she was growing up, it was Grandma who was the disciplinarian in the family. Grandpa was great at telling stories and playing jokes on the kids, but never yelled or spanked his children.

Two old time favorite stories about Grandpa Schafer that have been told over and over again by his daughters go back to the dating years of his girls. Apparently, his daughter and nieces who lived with Grandma and Grandpa had a bad habit of coming home late from a date. To teach the girls a lesson, he applied one of several strategies. On one occasion, he rearranged the furniture in the house. When the girls walked through the front door they immediately took off their shoes so know one would hear them. But to their surprise, they were bumping into and tripping over furniture that caused quite a noise and a ruckus. On another occasion when the girls were late getting home, Grandpa decided to go into their bedroom and hide under one of the beds. The girls quietly tip-toed into the house and eventually made it safely into the bedroom without tripping over any furniture. One of the girls turned on the bedroom light, another whispered, "I think this time we are safe." All of a sudden, the three girls looked down at the floor and saw a pair of big bare feet sticking out from one of the beds. They immediately let out a loud shriek and went screaming into Grandma and Grandpa's bedroom stating, "a stranger was hiding in their bedroom underneath one of the beds." The girls, of course, were furious when they learned that this was another one of their father's pranks.

When these two strategies failed to get the message across to his girls, Ben Schafer employed another, but also a very embarrassing strategy that finally worked. Like a good father, he stayed up until the girls arrived home from their dates. As soon as the boy friends' cars pulled up in the drive way, he went out to the car in his pajamas to escort his girls into the house. Bingo, no more good night kisses. Total humiliation and embarrassment followed for the girls who lived at Ben Schafer's house.

SEVERAL SIDE NOTES.

Ruby Schafer was one of four sisters. Her mother died at an early age. Ruby ended up raising her youngest sister, Helen. Aunt Helen was nine years younger than Grandma. Aunt Helen was living with Grandma and Grandpa when they were renting a house near Gonzaga University. During this time Aunt Helen became very good friends with the Crosby brothers. I am referring to both Bing and Bob. Grandma (the staunch Methodist) highly disapproved of the boys. She said they were smokers, drinkers and carousers. This did not discourage Aunt Helen from maintaining a friendship and dating the boys. Their friendship lasted a life time. Whenever Bing or Bob came to Spokane for a visit, Aunt Helen was sure to get a phone call and a visit from her old buddies.

Ben Schafer was known for the beautiful begonias that he grew in his greenhouse in his back yard on 17th. Ben also started the Orchid Society in Spokane, and belonged to numerous garden clubs.

ERIC AND ERNA BERT

Eric Box Bax van Werald, a Dutchman was born in Holland around the mid 1880's. He came to America as a young man seeking adventure and excitement. He left Holland not on the best of terms.

As a young man Eric loved the Theater and fell in love with a young budding actress. When he learned that the beautiful woman was pregnant with his child, he secretly married the starlet. When his wealthy and influential Dutch family learned about the marriage, they were outraged. In the eyes of his noble mother and father, Eric had disgraced his family by marrying the young actress. His parents did not disapprove of his love for the theater or having promiscuous affairs with young women. They did, however, believe it would be disgraceful to the family to marry someone who was not an aristocratic equal. Thespians in Eric's younger years (1900) in Europe were considered to be lower class citizens. Eric's family owned many of the shipping yards in Holland, and had acquired vast wealth and fortune. They didn't want Eric squandering the family's money on someone of lesser means.

Angry with his noble and wealthy family, Eric left Holland and moved to America.

At this point I do not know if the young actress accompanied Eric to America or if they had their marriage annulled. Growing up, I never heard Eric or my parents mention her name. She always remained a mystery to me, as well as, many aspects of Eric's early life in Holland and in America. What I do know is that Eric loved the fast life and the theater. He found the city of New York and Broadway to be exciting and exhilarating. To support himself he picked up odd jobs as a stage hand, helped to make stage sets, learned how valuable the lighting techniques were, and took small parts in various off-Broadway Theater, as well as, The Great White Way.

After spending a few years on the east coast where he developed a variety of stage skills, he found himself falling in love with the professional theater. The call of California, the lure of the motion picture studios and the possibility of making more money out west were beckoning him. To support himself along the way, he took on a variety of jobs. He worked in lumber mills, in the silver mines, waited tables and even worked as a cook. Eric, however, worked in the theater whenever the opportunity presented itself.

Eric did not fall in love with California like so many young Europeans did in the early 1920's. Work as an actor was competitive and hard to come by. After struggling for a couple of years as an actor, he became restless and decided to leave the state and look for work elsewhere. Eric loved to fish and hunt. He was told the Pacific Northwest was a sportsman's paradise and the land of opportunity. He headed north to the state of Washington, and settled in Spokane. When he arrived in Spokane he had with him his young son, Eric Junior. Financially, times were tough in Spokane during the late twenties, unless of course you were involved with the railroads, mining or lumbering. Being a stranger to the area and a single parent with a young lad to raise, he took on a variety of jobs. He worked in the Kellogg Mines, and in a brewery that was in downtown Spokane not too far from First Presbyterian Church. Eventually, he settled in Browne's Addition. During this time, Eric became involved in numerous theaters and musical groups' presentations in Spokane and the surrounding communities. The love and passion for the arts was truly in his blood.

It was while he was in Spokane that he met a beautiful blonde Danish photographer, named Erna Bert Nelson, who also shared an interest in the theater arts.

Erna Bert's father for many years owned a prestigious portrait photography business in Spokane. Mr. Nelson had three children, Harriet, Erna Bert, and Kenneth. All three children remained in Spokane and shared their fathers love for the camera. As adults, each one eventually started their own photography business.

In 1929, *The Spokane Woman* wrote a feature story about Erna Bert and her younger sister, Harriet. The article stated that Erna Bert's love for photography was handed down to her from her father, her grandfather and her great grandfather. She acquired the skills and art by serving as an apprentice in Denmark, where she learned the art of retouching. She believed that the art of portrait work was more important than painting. Erna Bert managed her parents' business at 824 ½ Riverside.

Erna Bert was a Soroptimist. While attending Washington State College in Pullman, she majored in drama and made a name for herself in the little theater movement of Spokane. Erna Bert gave her interpretation of Nora in "The Doll House." She played the part of Olivia in "Mr. Palm Passes By," and the part of Molly Gwynn in "Galsworth's Joy."

Both Eric and Erna Bert met when they were living in Browne's Addition and taking part in one of Spokane's theatrical productions. Their love for the arts and the outdoors enhanced their friendship. Before long, a wonderful courtship took place, and Eric proposed to Erna Bert. Following their marriage, Eric assisted Erna Bert with her portrait photography business and Erna Bert helped to raise Eric Jr.

Eric Jr. was the apple of his parents' eyes. He was a tall handsome boy with wavy blonde hair and light blue eyes. When young Eric grinned, his smile would go from ear to ear. He had an easy going personality, did very well in school and enjoyed learning photography. As he grew older, he would often assist Eric and Erna Bert with various photography assignments.

Eric Jr. and my father, Jack Magney, met when they attended Browne elementary school together. Even though Eric Jr. was several years older than Dad, they developed a friendship and periodically played together in Coeur d'Alene Park. As they grew older, they each attended Lewis and Clark High School where they played on the football team. Like most young people following graduation, these fine young men went separate directions. Both, however, did go on to college,, and both were in a college ROTC program. Jack joined the Army, and Eric Jr. enlisted in the Air Force.

When World War II broke out, Jack was commissioned a second Lieutenant in the Army and sent to the South Pacific where he served in the 161st

Infantry Regiment. Eric Jr. became an Air Force pilot who was also stationed in the South Pacific. At the end of the war, Jack returned home to his wife and family who all resided in Spokane. Eric Jr's. fate was much different. Early into the war in the South Pacific, Lt. Eric van Werald Jr. was on a night raid when his airplane was shot down. Neither Eric, nor his plane, was ever recovered.

The news of Eric Jr's death devastated Eric Sr. and Erna Bert. To help heal their aching wounds they decided the time was right to expand their growing photography business. For a number of years, they had been outgrowing the small photography studio that was in their home. In order for them to expand, they would need to relocate to a larger home.

Sadly, by the early 1940's, the Browne's Addition area was no longer the prestigious place to live. City fathers had slowly been moving away from this once upper class neighborhood of Spokane.

By 1917, the South Side or the "South Hill" was expanding. This was now the area where the wealthy were building their new homes, and was rapidly becoming the prominent place to reside. To Eric and Erna Bert's delight, they found the perfect home on the South Hill from which they could operate their photography business and have their private residence. It was near Manito Park, on the corner of Bernard and 22nd Street. The home was a three story, 3200 square feet colonial home built in 1923, with an unattached one car garage that was located to the back of the house on the east corner. Since the house occupied two city lots. Erna Bert could use the lot for her love of gardening and horticulture. A special attraction of this new home was the magnificent gardens that graced the back yard. There was a fish pond, lily ponds, rock gardens, rose gardens and space for entertaining their friends and family.

Eric and Erna Bert turned the first floor of the home into an elaborate portrait studio. In the back of the house, on the first floor, was a room for storing chemicals. Next to this room was the dark room where negatives were developed and some of the retouching of photographs took place. In the front of the house, as you entered the front door and turned to the left, was the business office where appointments were made and the bills paid. It was also the area to store the picture frames, paper and art supplies. The surface work for negatives and retouching of photographs was done in this area, as well as where wedding albums were assembled and senior pictures and baby pictures were mounted and framed.

To the right of the front entry was a spacious living room, filled with the cameras, screens, backdrops, lights and all the professional photography equipment that was needed to make life-like portraits. A gorgeous white built in artificial fireplace served as a dramatic backdrop. Numerous chairs, love seats, and a beautiful piano that was often played by her clients and used in her portraits, were also in this room. During the winter months when it was too cold to host a lavish dinner party in the rock garden or rose garden, Eric and Erna Bert would host many of their famous dinner parties in this room. At the ripe old age of five or six when Eric and Erna Bert were hosting one of their lavish parties, I was introduced to one of Eric's friends in this room; the jazz great Mr. Duke Ellington.

In the art studio, which was at the far East end of the house, sat a large elegant French Provincial cherry wood desk. This was where the clients would graciously be seated so they could study their negatives, chose their pictures, select their frames or see the completed portrait creations. Every wall was filled with recent, as well as some of the first portraits of Erna Bert's clients. Some of the portraits were in black and white, some in gold tone, but most were in heavy oils. There were portraits of brides, pictures of babies, and pictures of politicians like former Speaker of the House Thomas Foley. You could also see large family portraits of many of Spokane's prominent and wealthy families hanging next to pictures of Eric and Erna Bert.

The upstairs (second and third floor) were the living quarters. The kitchen was directly at the top of the stairs. The kitchen was of average size, large enough to have a table and four chairs that were placed in front of a large picture window that was 8 feet by 12 feet. It was in this room that Eric and Erna Bert could relax while eating and enjoy a panoramic view of their back yard rose garden, lily ponds, Bernard Street and Manito Park. It was also from the van Werald kitchen that Eric would monitor my arrival time from school.

To the right of the stairs was a long living room. The magnificent feature of this room was the even larger floor to ceiling window that provided a panoramic view of the backyard gardens and the future Japanese Tea Gardens of Manito Park.

The furniture was a mixture of elegant old English, delicate Queen Anne, modern or contemporary. At the far end of the room was a ceiling-to-floor book case that spanned the entire length of the wall. In that corner, Eric had a special wing back chair that sat next to a small table. On the table sat a wire recorder. This recorder was used to tape actors who were rehearsing for plays or musicals in Spokane.

The living quarters had a second piano that was often played by their well known and talented artsy friends who would come to socialize. The staircase that went to the third floor was very steep and narrow. Here were two additional bedrooms left unfinished and unoccupied.

By the time Eric and Erna Bert moved into their new home, most of the lots on the street had been developed, with the exception of three regular size lots and one extremely large vacant lot that sat on a massive basalt boulder and extended from 22nd Street to 23rd.

Following the death of Eric Jr. and the end of World War II, Eric and Erna Bert had become well known citizens of Spokane. Erna Bert was widely known and respected for her beautiful portrait photography business. Anybody who was anybody in Spokane would only allow Erna Bert to photograph them and their family. She was also making a name for herself in the horticulture scene. Her new passion in gardening was developing new strains of irises and roses. She absolutely adored living near Manito Park, Duncan Gardens and Rose Hill. When she was not working in the studio, she could be seen in the early hours of the day weeding her flower bed or pruning her roses.

Eric was also expanding his horizons. He was going back to his main passion, the theater. When he lived in New York and California, he made friends with new and struggling artists. Throughout the years he maintained his friendship with those individuals, many of whom remained in the theater throughout their lifetime and became famous. They encouraged Eric to continue his involvement with the theater arts in Spokane. He co-produced Kiss

Eric and Erna Bert's home and photography studio
on the corner of 22nd and Bernard

Left: Erna Bert Nelson in her garden on 22nd Street. Right: Eric Bax van
Werald on one of his duck hunting trips.

Me Kate, and was involved with other plays and musicals. Eric developed friendships with talented Spokanite artists such as Dorothy Darby Smith, a wonderful drama teacher, director, and part founder of the Spokane Civic Theater.

Eric's other passion was the out-of-doors. He was an avid sportsman who loved to hunt and fish. He purchased acres of land by Moses Lake known as the Potholes. To add to his love for hunting and fishing, he decided to raise and train Labrador Retrievers. It was at the Potholes that he would train his dogs in the fine art of retrieving ducks, pheasants, and geese that would fall from the sky. At home, Eric constructed a super size dog house and dog run for his Labrador Retrievers. As days and years passed by for Eric, his loving and ever obedient dogs such as King and Valentine became his children.

By the end of World War II, Eric and Erna Bert's names were often in print, and periodically the Spokane newspapers would write feature stories about the couple. The van Werald/Nelson home of 22nd Street had acquired special distinctions and notoriety. The home was by far a more sumptuous and larger structure than the typical smaller bungalow rambler-styled homes that existed on the short street. The lavish landscaping and the magnificent flower beds afforded this home a more impressive appearance than the other homes.

A SIDE NOTE.

Erna Bert continued to live in the Colonial home many years following Eric's sudden death in 1964. Several years after Erna Bert passed away, the city parks department erected an archway on Rose Hill in memory of Erna Bert and her contributions to the Gardens Clubs and the Rose Society of Spokane.

SPOKANE FOLLOWING WW II

Spokane, Washington, was the home of two major reserve units at the outset of the war. The 161st Infantry Regiment of the Washington National Guard, which drew rifle companies from throughout eastern Washington, fought in Guadalcanal, New Georgia, and Luzon and eventually took part in the occupation of Japan.

The 14th Marine Corps Reserve Battalion was called into active service a year before the onset of the war. This unit was divided up and its members scattered throughout the Pacific.

At the end of World War II, about 10,000 GIs from these and other armed force units returned to their hometown of Spokane, and gradually found work. Economically, the country was booming, but places to live were difficult to find, and veterans with their families lived in cramped apartments, bought trailers and parked them in someone's back yard, or lived with parents. Rapidly, new housing developments sprang up in many parts of the city. The GI Bill and no-down payment terms meant almost anyone could buy a house. Fields on the north side of town that had been empty all of a sudden had rows of little 800 square- foot pastel houses. On the south side of town, vacant lots that were sprinkled throughout existing streets and neighborhoods were now sucked up by contractors and builders. Quickly, new homes were constructed and co-mingled with the older existing south side homes. This was a true example of the house on 22nd Street that Jack and Dorothy Magney would eventually build. The majority of the homes on 22nd Street had been built in the 1920s and 30s.

According to author William Stimson in his book, *Spokane A View Of The Falls,* "Spokane emerged from the war with a revitalized economy. The aluminum plants at Mead and Trentwood were purchased from the federal government by ex-Spokanite Henry J. Kaiser and began supplying modern metals to the private manufacturing companies around the globe."

"The Army Air Depot (where Dorothy worked during the war) located west of Airway Heights was renamed Fairchild Air Force Base in 1950, and became a permanent installation. Geiger Field, the landing strip partially built by the city just prior to the war and completed by the Army Air Corps, was returned to the city of Spokane following World War II. City and county officials decided the most practical way to make use of the air strip was to build a public airport."

In the late forties and the early fifties, Spokane saw the city follow a pattern of decentralization. Changes in transportation were a major factor in altering the central area. More people than ever began owning their own cars and did not depend on the bus system. In the 1950's, President Eisenhower's administration initiated plans to significantly improve our nation's highway system by building a new interstate freeway systems across America. Automobile travel increased, and large trucks began transporting freight on this new highway system. Car manufacturers designed faster and larger automobiles. Gasoline was cheap to purchase. New roads made travel and transportation easier and affordable. Life in Spokane became a middle class life style, a new reality for many after the war.

As people traveled more by car, motels began to spring up in Spokane. These motels were usually constructed near the new highways and interstates. This was true when Spokane saw the creation and expansion of Interstate 90. Many of the downtown hotels, such as the famous Davenport and Spokane Hotel, found it hard to compete for business. In Spokane and elsewhere, the new motel concept began to flourish and expand. A classic example of this was the new Spokane House, which had a panoramic view of downtown Spokane and was built near Sunset Highway.

The history of business is an important aspect of Spokane's past and present. Agriculture, banking, colleges and universities, the hospitality industry, manufacturing, the military, the medical community, publishing, and the retail industry all played a vital role in the growth and expansion of the city of Spokane during the 1950's.

In 1949, Harry Cooper started his Produce Supply Company. Harry had two innovations that became well known: one was Eddies Salad Mix and the other was with potatoes. Harry developed a technique to sell ready-to-cook hash browns. Grandpa Schafer worked for URM Distributors and ended up being a promoter of these two innovations.

In the 1950s R.A. Pearson built a machine that used vacuum-operated suction cups to set up card board six-pack bottle carriers. His device was an instant success. Eventually he built packaging machines designed for food and beverage containers and other products.

The Spokane Steel Foundry was started by John C. Tenold in 1952. It became the sole supplier of replacement track roller guards for the Caterpillar Tractor Company.

Raymond Hanson, invented an automatic leveler for combines that contained a mercury switch. He successfully convinced farmers and equipment manufactures to purchase his invention. This invention, later contributed to his success on a Columbia River water reclamation project in the mid 1950s.

A good friend to Jack and Dorothy was Eric A. Johnston, a well known civic leader and owner of Columbia Electric and Manufacturing. After the war, the company designed and manufactured fluorescent fixtures. In the late 1950's, Columbia developed recessed fluorescent light fixtures using Corning glass. This allowed Columbia Lighting to become a leader in the production of the fluorescent lighting market.

Another popular industry that had originated in Spokane in the 50s was American Sign and Indicator. The successful business was started by Luke and Chuck Williams. The brothers invented signs that would light up and flash changing messages and pictures. Today these signs are now considered ordinary and are widespread. They are seen in ball parks, on billboards, in banks etc. all across the globe.

Banking became an even bigger business in Spokane in the 50s. One of the largest and most well known banking institutions was the Washington

Trust Company (Bank) where Jesse Groff my uncle, worked for many years as a branch manager, eventually working into the position of one of the Vice Presidents of Commercial Loans. The Washington Trust Company was founded in Spokane in 1902. The bank thrived under the leadership of Fredrick Stanton and Martin Connelly. As an example, in 1950, Washington Trust became the first bank in Spokane and the Inland Empire to open a drive-in branch. A year later the firm was officially renamed Washington Trust Bank.

The medical community played an important role in Spokane in the early history of the city in the fifties. Due to its geographical location, two church related hospitals were started in the early history of Spokane. One hospital was started by the Deaconesses who were affiliated with the Methodist Church, and the other hospital was started by the Sisters of Providence who belonged to the Roman Catholic Church.

In January, 1892, the first Deaconess Board of Directors was organized in the Pacific Northwest. Like many Hospitals in early America, the leadership and sponsorship came from church organization. The Deaconesses were mission driven lay people from the Methodist Church. The Chicago Methodist Training School taught the Deaconess how to care for people who were living in the slums. According to the *Deaconess Story 1896 to 1996* written by Priscilla Gilkey, Margaret Crabtree and Terren Roloff; in 1896 when a group of Deaconesses were preparing breakfast, a stranger arrived at the home in need of medical help. The Deaconesses turned the kitchen table into an operating table and the stove became the sterilizing department. Dr. George Libby performed an appendectomy on the man.

The book continues to state that Spokane resident Minnie Beard O'Neill was extremely interested in the work the Deaconesses performed. She wanted to see their work grow and continue, but lacked the finances to donate to the important mission. Minnie was a devoted Christian lady and asked God to help her husband Franklin, a miner, locate a mine of significant value. With the money from the mine, she would tithe assets to build a hospital for the Deaconesses. As Franklin went in search of the mine, Minnie remained at home and prayed that God would honor her request. Franklin Beard located such a mine in Sandon, B.C. and later sold it for $50,000. Minnie remained true to her covenant with God and donated $5,000 to start a hospital. In April 1896, the Maria Beard Deaconess Home of Spokane was incorporated. Maria Beard was the mother of Minnie Beard O'Neil. The people involved with the incorporation agreed that the purpose was: "to provide instruction in the Bible and all that pertains to home and foreign mission work; to give practical training to city mission work; to give such aid to missionaries as may be practicable; to employ Deaconesses, instructors and nurses, and as incidental to objects and purposes, to establish and maintain a suitable Christian home or homes."

The first official hospital was a thirty foot high building with 20 rooms and was erected facing Fourth between Howard and Mill Streets.

The school of nursing for the hospital opened in 1899. Six students were admitted to the program that would eventually graduate over 2,000 nurses. Through the years, the hospital grew by leaps and bounds.

The fifties brought dramatic changes to the hospital and to medicine. In June, 1952, The Spokesman Review reported; "Ralph Berg, Jr., MD, a Spokane chest surgeon, opened the heart valve of a Fairfield, Washinton woman in a dramatic first surgery of its kind. The surgeon put his finger inside the heart of a 26-year-old woman for three minutes and added years to her life as a result."

Plastic heart valves were developed that year and by the late 50s many patients at Deaconess Hospital, and throughout the United States, were receiving them as part of their medical treatment.

Other modern medical miracles were taking place in Spokane and across the globe. The first use of radioactive iodine was in 1953. The vaccine for polio was discovered by Dr. Jonas E. Salk. School children throughout American and in Spokane, including this author, were given the vaccine in the public school system.

In 1954, Deaconess announced it would build a $1,100,000, five-story addition. The new wing opened in sections in 1955. Another addition was built in 1957 and named Sherwood Hall. In 1956, The Deaconess Auxiliary was formed.

Sacred Heart Hospital was another of the prominent hospitals in Spokane in the 50s. This hospital was started by the Sisters of Providence, who arrived in the territory in 1856. Mother Joseph and her Sisters of Providence worked as pioneer caregivers, establishing schools and hospitals.

William Stimson in his book *Spokane a View of the Falls,* states "in 1887, Sacred Heart Hospital opened with 31 beds to serve the town's 3,000 people. In 1888, the hospital had a medical staff of six and added a wing doubling its bed count. In 1947, the Sisters started a nursing school at the hospital, and in 1950, established physical therapy and emergency departments. In 1959, the first open heart surgery was performed at the hospital."

The Rockwood Clinic was started in the 1930s, by Spokanite, Dr. William W. Robinson. Following WWII, Dr. Robinson began recruiting his colleagues to join him in a new style of medicine, the "group practice." By today's standards, this is a very common and accepted way to practice medicine. During the fifties the "group practice" was a new concept, and many doctors shied away from that form of practicing medicine.

The educational communities in Spokane also experienced a period of growth and expansion. Private Christian schools such as Whitworth College and Gonzaga University were part of this process. Both educational centers are located on the north side of Spokane. Whitworth College is located on Hawthorne Road between Wall and North Division. The college was named after a Presbyterian Pastor, George W. Whitworth. In 1890, he founded Summer Academy, a Christian college that was eventually named Whitworth College and relocated to Spokane. Dr. Whitworth organized the First Presbyterian Church of Seattle, and was the third President of the University of Washington. Gonzaga University is a large campus situated near the Spokane River, not far from North Division and Boone, and close to St. Aloysius Parish. The University is known for having an outstanding athletic department and a well known law schools. The University operated under the founding leadership of the Jesuit Priests.

The GI Bill enabled many returning soldiers to enter college and seek a higher education. Both Whitworth and Gonzaga saw their collegiate enrollments grow rapidly.

In 1950, Dr. Frank Warren was the President of Whitworth College. He and the Board of Trustees promoted Whitworth's Presbyterian heritage and identity.

During this time, Whitworth developed outstanding athletic, music and educational programs. This was accomplished by elevating its academic standards by hiring well known Christian scholars and professors such as Dr. Clarence Simpson and Dr. Clinton Duvall.

Gonzaga in the fifties was also enhancing its academic and sports programs. The university's School of Law already had one of the best reputations in the country. Following the war, this small Jesuit University located on the Spokane River was growing rapidly.

In Spokane, education was considered to be important to children of all ages, not just for the high school graduate. Private Catholic elementary and high schools had always played an important role in education. A great emphasis was placed on the shoulders of Catholic parents, regarding the importance of raising their children in the Roman Catholic Church, where they would receive a superior education. Following the war, this belief became even more pronounced. While the Roman Catholics were strengthening and enhancing their educational curriculum, a new wave of private education to Protestant children began to grab hold.

Several Lutheran churches in Spokane in the 50s began offering private elementary classes to any family interested and willing to pay the high cost.

On the north side of Spokane, a number of Protestant churches, Baptist, Nazarene, Assembly of God and several Pentecostal churches believed God was directing them to begin the formation of a Christian School that would have its own campus away from any of the founding or sponsoring churches. A board of directors was formed, and land was purchased on Central in between Wall and Cedar. The new school became known as Northwest Christian School.

Growth and expansion were taking place in Spokane's downtown district. A new Newberry's store was built on the corner of Howard and Riverside in 1952. In 1953, J.C. Penney built a department store on Main and Post.

The Crescent Department store built a new addition in 1956, and in

1957, the Bon Marche, on Main and Stevens, built their new addition.

The Crescent Department Store was my favorite store. Here one could spend the entire day shopping, eating, or meeting friends and family under the clock near the escalators. The Crescent was the best place in town to enjoy the merriment and ambiance of the Christmas spirit.

Little did I realize in the fifties that one day I would become an employee of this splendid department store. It was here that I learned about the world of retail merchandising, the importance of offering excellent customer service, and good business management practices. Because the Crescent played such an important role in my life, I want to give some detailed history about this famous Spokane business.

The store actually had its grand opening August 5, 1889. In the twenty-four hours preceding the stores grand opening, most of the city's business district had burned to the ground. Robert B. Paterson and his partner Captain J. M. Comstock, the owners of the department store were newcomers to Spokane's business community. Mr. Paterson was sent by Captain Comstock to Spokane to arrange for sixteen-by-ninety-foot quarters in the newly constructed Crescent Block, just east of the Spokesman Review building which the great fire spared. Within two years following the great fire, Captain Comstock added two valued employees from Iowa, James L. Paine and Eugene A. Shadle, who joined Mr. Paterson in Spokane.

The Crescent purchased sixty-eight feet of land at Riverside and Wall in June 1898, and commenced the construction of its own building. In 1903, it acquired facilities on Main Street for a wholesale house, the Spokane Dry Goods Co.

In its first 10 years, the Crescent had four different locations. By 1909, The Crescent employed three hundred people. Further expansion was necessary, and in 1917, adjacent land on the corner of Main and Wall was purchased. The seven story building was completed in 1919. The Crescent survived the lean years of the Great Depression and operated as a family-owned business. In 1944, the baton was passed from father to son when Robert A. Patterson became the general manager.

According to the store's teaching literature which was distributed to all new employees, early in the history of the store, The Crescent adopted the philosophy of "peace for all." This was a mercantile concept that originated in 1837 in New Castle England. The idea was practiced in the east coast by A.T. Wanamaker and by Marshall Field as a way to be fair to a customer and not haggle over prices. The purpose was to give business stability, and be removed from the customary bickering of a bazaar. Crescent executives demanded the store employees treat the customer with high respect and provide excellent service. Everything was done to adjust any problem the customer might have. The Crescent merchandizing theory was, "the customer is always right."

Additional retail growth and expansion was also occurring on the north side of town on Division, between Wellsley and Queen. Land had been purchased and the construction of Spokane's first shopping mall was taking place. This new shopping wonder was named Northtown. The grand opening occurred in December of 1954 and consisted of eight stores. For many years the new mall struggled. The best feature of this new mall was all of the free parking. The mall was a favorite place for the families who resided on the north side of Spokane but for the more affluent families who resided on the South Hill, there was much skepticism as to the success of the mall. Many residents who lived on the South Side preferred the convenience of shopping at The Crescent and the Bon Marche in the heart of downtown Spokane.

Near Grand and 29th, on the South Hill, was a cluster of small family owned businesses. This section was referred to as the Manito shopping area and encompassed an area of four to five blocks. The majority of the store owners lived within a couple of miles from their businesses. Families who owned businesses in the Manito Shopping district were very involved with their churches, schools, and took an active roll in the political life of this small community. For people who lived on the South Hill, there was no reason to consider shopping on the North side of Spokane. The small mom and pop shops in Manito were close to home, free parking was available, and the friendship of the store owners couldn't be beat. There was exciting news that expansion, including an Ernst Hardware store along with a Rosauer's supermarket, was to be built on 29th in the Manito shopping area.

Following World War II, life for the citizens of Spokane was bright and promising. There was continuous growth and development wherever anyone looked. Jobs could be found by most every one who wanted to work. The GI Bill enabled returning veterans the opportunity to further their education, and purchase new homes for their young growing families. Spokane in the early and mid fifties became a thriving and growing place to live.

A SPECIAL SIDE NOTE.

Meet Me Under The Clock

An important landmark in Spokane when I was growing up in the fifties was a huge brown stained, cube sided clock that hung from the ceiling on the first floor of The Crescent, by the escalator. I realize it might seem unusual to consider a clock a landmark, but this clock played a very significant role in the lives of all Spokanites. When downtown and planning on meeting someone the most popular comment was to say "meet me under the clock." Meeting under the clock referred to this familiar location at The Crescent Department Store. The clock had four faces and was about 36 square inches on each side. The clock was not ornate or fancy. It was a basic and simple mission style. A circle framed the face of very large, easy-to-read numbers. I am not sure why the citizens of Spokane chose this location to meet family, friends or business associates. I do know that it was a tradition that was

The Crescent Clock decorated for the holidays

established many years before I was born.

The Crescent was a wonderful place to eat a delicious meal at the fountain, the men's grill or the ladies Tea Room. It was also a favorite store to purchase flowers or special gifts. The location of the store was in the heart and center of downtown Spokane, which was a trouble-free place to make contact with someone.

Three great memories I have of the department store as a child were; the clock, the ladies Tea Room where my cousin Karen and I enjoyed lunch and a fashion show; and the beautifully decorated Crescent display windows, especially at Christmas time. There were four huge windows that faced Main Street. The store hired a team of display artists who continually changed the windows as new merchandise arrived. The displays were always a work of art. The main intent was to promote and sell the store's merchandise. Christmas was my favorite time to view the magical window display. One never knew what the theme would be for the holiday season. We always knew the main feature would be Santa Claus. Some seasons, the theme would be about Santa

One of the Crescent Department Stores lavish Christmas display window scenes.

and his elves. Other times it would be about the reindeer or the animals that lived in the forest by the North Pole. People of all ages were mesmerized by the fantasy of The Crescent window display. Daily crowds congregated at the windows, and soaked up the wonder and beauty of the Christmas season.

Today, there are no more Crescent window displays. The ladies tea room, the soda fountain and the Men's Grill are long gone. The Crescent Store was sold to Fredrick and Nelson. Following many years of owning and managing the aged Crescent Building, Fredrick and Nelson sold the store. Sadly, Fredrick and Nelson and all other future owners did not take the interest in the grand old building or the founder's concept for retailing. As time marched forward and new shopping malls blossomed in the outer regions, shoppers did not stop to look at the window displays. As young American women sought careers in the work force, they did not have the time to spend attending classy fashion shows in the Tea Room. Spokanites were now visiting new shopping malls which provided lots or free parking space. No longer were shoppers saying those magical words that had been stated for four or more generations, "meet me under the clock."

Eventually, The Crescent building was sold to a Spokane firm known as Goodale and Barbieri. The new owners of this famous Spokane landmark were modern visionaries. They hired clever and talented craftsmen and re-modeled the old structure. Today, the old Crescent building is now known as the Crescent Court, where small businesses now occupy much of the space, along with several eateries.

I had the good fortune to talk with Cal Brown who manages the Crescent Court, and Jonathon Bixby who restored the old clock. According to these gentlemen, the Crescent actually had an eighth floor that was used for a wood working shop. To most Spokanites and employees of the Crescent everyone believed the store had only seven floors. It was on this eighth floor that store counters were made, and decorations for the window displays were stored and created. It was also in this room that the original clock was made. Jon was given the task of restoring the old clock and building a replica clock. The replica hangs from the second floor of the Crescent Court. Jon said the wood for the original clock was made out of a high quality oak called Cortisone

Oak. The mechanisms of the clock were electric and divided into four sections with a metal liner, and back lit to make the black lettering on the clock stand out.

Next time you are in downtown Spokane, plan on meeting someone for lunch at the Crescent Court. Before you eat that meal, first arrange to meet "under the clock at the Crescent."

ADDITIONAL SIDE NOTE.

In 1948 a family friend, confidant and physician, Dr. Elizabeth White was elected president of the Deaconess Medical Staff at their annual meeting. She was the first woman to hold this position. She was a graduate of Lewis and Clark High School, and received her doctorate degree from Iowa State. She began her practice in Spokane in 1937.

1953 marked a high point for the Magney, Schafer families and for Dr. Elizabeth White. On April 14 and 15, she was busy delivering babies for two sisters, Dorothy Magney and Virginia Groff. On the 14th, Virginia delivered a son, Kevin, and on the 15th, Janice was born to Jack and Dorothy. Janice and Kevin would be the last babies Dr. White would deliver for our families, but the long friendship between Dr. White and Dorothy continued for many years.

Deaconess Hospital played a prominent role in the lives of the Magney and Schafer family. Both Jack and Dorothy were born in this hospital in 1917. Many years later, their daughter-in-law, Lynn Magney, would be very involved with the management of the medical lab.

Dad was a long time admirer of Dr. Robinson, founder of the Rockwood Clinic. He so badly wanted mom to make a change and join this expanding clinic that currently has medical clinics throughout Spokane and the Spokane Valley. Mom, however, remained ever faithful to Dr. White.

REMBERING THE FIFTIES

During the 50s, life was pretty much the same in Spokane as it was throughout the rest of America. The locations of cities, towns and states may be different but the people shared the same common threads, the love for family, church and pride in America. Each generation, however, will leave behind certain memories that will distinguish it from other generations. This is true for how I remember certain aspects of the 50s and life in Spokane.

Here are just a few special memories that I think readers may find amusing and entertaining. They are highlights from an era that no longer exists except in history books and old newspaper clippings.

- Nearly everyone's mom was at home when the kids got home from school.
- Most moms did not work outside the home. They did, however, work hard volunteering their time at the schools their children attended and at the churches where they had their membership.
- Moms wore nylons that came in two pieces and were held up by garter belts. (During the war when nylons were among the many things difficult or impossible to buy, moms and all women drew penciled lines down the backs of their bare legs to simulate the line that would otherwise be on their stockings.)
- Going out to dinner with parents was a thrill for most children, not an everyday occurrence.
- Being sent to the Principal's office was nothing compared to the fate that awaited us at home. Our parents and grandparents were

a far greater threat. Having their approval was of great importance.

❦ All the male teachers wore white shirts and neckties. The female teachers wore high heel shoes, long skirts, blouses or dresses and had their hair styled at the beauty shop.

❦ Moving forward a grade was not an automatic thing. Parents and teachers threatened to hold us kids back a grade if we failed. They did exactly that if a child did not measure up.

❦ We never had to lock the front door or the car door. No one ever asked where the car keys were, because they were always in the car ignition.

❦ Gasoline cost 20 to 30 cents a gallon. When we stopped for gas at Jack Devine's Service station on 3rd Avenue, a gas station attendant came out to pump the gas, clean our windshield, check the oil and put air in the tires. We didn't pay extra for those services. Our family collected sets of juice and water glasses that were often given away if you purchased the required amount of gas. Gas stations, like the grocery stores, gave free trading stamps. Trading stamp books could be redeemed for all kinds of merchandise. At the grocery store, those glasses and other prizes were often included in a box of laundry detergent.

❦ Almost everyone's dream car was the swept wing 1957 Chevy, especially if you were twenty or younger. Cruising down Riverside on a Friday evening was known as tooling Riverside. It was important to be seen riding in the latest Chevy that hit the car dealership!

❦ Across the street from Roosevelt Grade School on Bernard was a candy store called Mike's. For a few pennies, we could buy wax coke-shaped bottles with colored sugar water inside, candy cigarettes, black jack, clove and teaberry chewing gum. If you were fortunate enough to have five cents, you could buy a pack of baseball cards.

❦ Bottles of Coke were 6 oz., and bottles of Pepsi were 12 oz. Both, however, cost the same.

- Milk was delivered by the milk man in a milk delivery truck throughout the neighborhood. First thing in the morning, I would open the front door and find milk in glass bottles. There was always a thick layer of heavy cream on the top of the bottles.
- The bakery man also drove a truck and delivered breads, cakes, cookies and pies to the house.
- The Fuller Brush man stopped by the house to sell brushes and cleaning supplies.
- Refrigerators had metal ice cubes trays with levers. The refrigerators had to be defrosted every other month or there would be a build up of ice in the freezer.
- Telephone numbers consisted of seven numbers and the prefix was the name of a person or street, such as Riverside (747-6622).
- We all wore P.F. Fliers, had roller skate keys, collected 45 RPM records and played with peashooters or cork pop guns.
- Drive Ins were movie theaters that were opened in the summer months only. The other Drive In was a hamburger restaurant. A waitress on roller skates would come to your car window and take your order.
- Virtually everyone had a Hi-Fi in their home, or drove a Studebaker.
- We used typewriters and lots of carbon paper when preparing written material. At school, teachers handed out mimeograph paper. To make a correction on a carbon copy, a single edged razor blade worked great! Parents volunteered their time to work in the school office and run the mimeograph machine.
- As kids, we played with tinker toys, erector sets, Fort Apache Play Sets, Lincoln Logs and paper dolls.
- If you were fortunate and there was a McDonald's in your home town, hamburgers cost 15 cents.
- A "Race Issue" meant arguing about who ran the fastest.
- Having a weapon in school meant being caught with a slingshot.
- Kids hoped all winter long for at least a foot of snow because that meant school might be closed.

❧ Girls wore ugly gym uniforms they all hated.

❧ Saturday morning cartoons weren't 30-minute commercials for action figures. It usually took about five minutes for the TV to warm up. The picture was only in black and white.

❧ Favorite TV shows for kids were The Lone Ranger, Hop Along Cassidy, The Mickey Mouse Club, Lassie Come Home, Rin-Tin-Tin, Buffalo Bob, Howdy Doody, the Peanut Gallery, and Roy Rogers and Dale Evans. Favorite books were Nancy Drew, and The Hardy Boys.

❧ The movie theaters showed two feature movies, a cartoon, and a newsreel. Children under the age of 12 got in for 10 cents.

❧ The 50s saw the beginnings of rock and roll. Within every American household, there was much discussion about Elvis Presley and his two hit songs: *Blue Suede Shoes* and *You Ain't Nothin But a Hound Dog.*

❧ Little Richard also caused a stir and commotion with his big hit *Good Golly Miss Molly.* Dean Martin sold millions of *Memories Are Made of This.* The McGuire sisters had a hit tune called *Sincerely.* Pat Boone became famous for his *Love Letters In the Sand.* And cowboy star and singer, Gene Autry, recorded two Christmas songs that remain classics today: *Frosty the Snowman* and *Rudolph the Red Nose Reindeer.*

❧ Catching fireflies could happily occupy an entire evening. Playing a game "Oly-oly-oxen-free" made perfect sense. Spinning around, getting dizzy, and falling down was cause for the giggles. Water balloons were the ultimate weapon in the summer.

❧ Lying on our backs in the grass besides our friends and saying,, "that cloud looks like a—" was a summer favorite among friends.

❧ We could play baseball without the help of adults. Hop Scotch, jumping rope, and tree climbing were fun games.

❧ The worst embarrassment in grade school was being picked last for kick ball or tug of war.

❧ Riding bicycles with our friends was great fun. More fun was putting baseball cards in the spokes of our bikes and pretending we were on souped up motorcycles.

❦ Twenty five cents was a terrific allowance!

❦ Pot was what Mom cooked the chili in.

❦ No one owned a purebred dog.

❦ A favorite saying was "I double dog dare ya."

Oh, for the good old days of the 50s! It was a time when neighbors said "Hi" to each other and looked after each other's children. Going to church was important. We were allowed to pray in the public schools. The words "Under God" were added to the Pledge of Allegiance. During the school week, classes were dismissed for a full hour so students could attend bible school. Stores and gas stations were closed on Sunday.

Spokane in the fifties was a time for building a new future, a new promise, and a new generation. I was part of that new generation. I was part of an era that has come and gone. Today, I am proud to be able to share with my children and my grandchildren some of the joys and delights that I experienced as a young person growing up in my beloved Spokane. A wonderful place to live — a place to explore, march in a parade, build a bomb shelter, pick huckleberries, swim in the lakes, play in the parks, and ride a roller coaster. It was a wonderful time!

JACK AND DOROTHY BUILD A HOUSE

Time does not erase the love for those who have been near and dear to us. Time did not erase the love that Eric and Erna Bert had for Eric Jr. But time did heal some scars and wounds that had been etched in their hearts. A new day and a new horizon were just around the corner for Eric and Erna Bert.

After World War II, Jack and Dorothy Magney made a crucial decision that would impact their entire married life. Jack loved the Army and the military life, but both Jack and Dorothy's aging parents lived in Spokane. If First Lt. Jack Magney was to remain as an active duty officer in the Army, he could be stationed any place in the United States or abroad. The big question was how could he serve his country and remain in active duty military, and live in Spokane? At the end of the war, the National Guard in downtown Spokane needed a full time active duty officer to assist other officers.

Subsequent to daily discussions, Jack and Dorothy believed God was opening up a window of opportunity for them. Jack placed two requests with the military: he asked to be transferred out of the Army and into the National Guard, and to be assigned to a full-time active duty officer position in Spokane's National Guard. Jack's requests were granted.

At the time that Jack put in his request for change, he and Dorothy were stationed in Cheyenne, Wyoming. I was a baby about a year old when my mother found herself expecting her second child.

The Spokane families were thrilled and elated to receive the news that Jack and Dorothy would be returning to Spokane, and making Spokane their permanent home.

Dad's father, C. A. Magney, offered a large two bedroom apartment to Jack and Dorothy in the Berkley apartment building. The Berkley apartments were located on Riverside, four blocks away from the Brunot Hall apartments.

When I was 13 months old, Mom and Dad bid their farewells to Cheyenne Wyoming, the Army, and moved to Spokane.

Quickly they settled into their two bedroom apartment in the Browne's Addition area of Spokane. Mom, like her mother Ruby Schafer, was a wonderful cook and homemaker and ecstatic to be back home with her close family and friends. She felt a sense of security being close to Dr. Elizabeth White. Dr. Elizabeth would now be delivering my new sibling into this world. Dad was settling into his new career as a full-time duty officer with the National Guard, and also welcoming the new opportunity to be near his aging parents.

Both Mom and Dad became actively involved with First Presbyterian Church. Dad sang in the choir and Mom, with insistence from Aunt Mary, joined the Lucia Pratt women's circle and the church women's association.

Mom was thrilled to be expecting her second child. At thirty years of age, mom delivered the Magney's second child. My brother, Richard Allen Magney, was a bouncing eight pound boy, born at Deaconess Hospital the day after Christmas in 1947.

By the time Richard was an active three year old boy, Jack and Dorothy realized that they had out grown the two bedroom apartment, and should be raising their children in a home with a nice yard and neighborhood.

The search began for either a new home or a piece of property so they could build. As luck would have it, they found both. Mom and Dad were put in touch with a realtor who was friends with a well-known builder who had just completed pouring the foundation of a house on the south side of Spokane near Manito Park. As yet, there were no buyers for the house, which sat next to a huge vacant lot that would probably go undeveloped for many years. This empty lot was on an enormous hill consisting of huge solid basalt rock boulders. The property was located on 22nd Street between Browne and Bernard.

After meeting with the builder, Jack and Dorothy fell in love with the floor plans. They believed this was the house and the location God had selected for them to raise their children. An offer was made, and some floor plans revised to meet Dorothy's specifications. The ultimate move-in goal was set for early summer or late spring of 1951.

A daily ritual for Eric van Werald was to walk his Labrador retrievers for a good twenty minutes, two times a day. Each morning he found time to stop and chit chat with the construction workers who were building this new home. On one particular occasion, as all four sides to the house were prepped for a paint job and the front door was being hung, Eric happened to have a discussion with the builder, Mr. Mom. He wanted to know if the house had been sold. Mr. Mom informed Eric the house had been sold to a young family with two small children. The oldest child would be starting Kindergarten at Roosevelt Grade School. The parents were in a hurry to get the house built, and hoped to be settled comfortably into their new home before the beginning of the new school year. The construction plans were to have the home finished by the first of June.

Continuing the conversation, Eric asked Mr. Mom if, by any chance, he knew the name of the young couple who would be moving into the house. He responded, "As a matter of fact, I do know their names. It's Jack and Dorothy Magney." Eric's eyes lit up in a flash. He asked for their phone number and explained to Mr. Mom that Jack and his late son Eric Jr. had been friends before and during the war and had attended the same elementary and high schools.

Mr. Mom responded, "I can do better than give you their phone number. The Magneys will be up here this afternoon to finalize some last minute changes and view the progress that has been made on the house. Come on over and greet your new neighbors."

Eric shook Mr. Mom's hand and assured him, he would be stopping by to say hello to Jack and meet his family.

The day was warm and balmy with temperatures in the seventies. The sky was a vibrant blue. Dad had just washed his 1950 two-door Ford Sedan, and Mom had put ribbons in my hair. I was fidgety and excited. Mom was yelling at Dad to hurry and finish with the car. It was time to leave. According to

71

Mom's memories, we were scheduled to meet with the builder of our new home at three o'clock. Yes, we were on our way to 22nd Street to visit our new home.

This would be my first trip to actually see our new home. I was extremely excited and highly energized. Mom had told me that I was going to have my very own bedroom. Wow! How exciting! My own bedroom! As for Richard, well, I don't think he had a clue as to why I was so overjoyed and antsy.

I can see it as if it were yesterday. Mom and Dad were standing in front of a wooden structured building that was being painted a drab color of green. According to today's color charts, this color would be known more as slate green, but to me, it was an ugly color of green. I was never sure why my mother selected this color for our home. Surrounding the house was nothing more than dirt on all sides and numerous trucks sat in front. To the left of the house was an enormous empty lot that was filled with giant trees, which seemed to me to reach way into the sky.

The trees sat on rocks that were bigger than the new green house that was going to become my home. Wow! This was awesome! Richard and I could climb trees and rocks. We would have our very own forest to play in whenever we wanted to be outside.

I remember Mom and Dad talking with a man who was wearing this strange belt that held a hammer and a bunch of other dangling tools.

These three grown-ups were deep in conversation when the largest man I had ever seen in my life walked up to my dad and put his big arms around him and said, "Jack, Eric van Werald, we haven't seen one another in many years and now I have learned that we are going to be neighbors."

I couldn't believe what I was seeing with my very own eyes! My daddy was being hugged by Santa Claus, or was it the giant from Jack and the Bean Stalk? I couldn't make up my mind as to which one. This man who called himself Eric certainly looked like Santa Claus to me. He had a big round belly, bright red cheeks, and a balding head with white wavy hair. But what he didn't have was long hair or a long white wavy beard. He did have a mustache, though.

Maybe he was the giant from Jack in the Bean Stalk. Mom had just read the story to Richard and I, and this man, Eric, had hands so huge they could have belonged to any giant. As my eyes focused upward, I realized I was seeing the most enormous man on earth.

As Eric towered over my father, the two men stood embracing one another, and then Dad stood back and said, "Eric let me introduce my wife, Dorothy." Once again this massive man wrapped his huge arms around my mother and said in a very thick Dutch accent, "Dorothy, you have no idea how wonderful it is to meet you. It has been many years since I have seen Jack. Now, he is here with a family and we are going to be neighbors. This is truly a great day for me and those who live on 22nd Street. I know we will be seeing a lot of one another."

Then suddenly he bent down to look Richard and me in the eye. This was *Scary! Scary! Scary!* I was either staring at Santa Claus or having eye to eye contact with the Giant from *Jack and the Bean Stalk*. With one big swoop, Eric had his giant arms wrapped around both Richard and me, and pulled us tightly to his big thick chest. I was so startled I didn't know what to do. He held us closely in his arms for what seemed like an eternity. When he finally let go, I noticed tears glittering in his big blue eyes. He gave Richard and me a big kiss and said, "When you move into your new home, I will come and visit you every day even if you are sick. We are going to be best friends. We will go for walks together. You can play with the dogs and when it rains, I will take you to school and pick you up." I was speechless and dumbfounded, but it sounded pretty good to me. Maybe this Eric was Santa Claus, or maybe even a brother to Santa. After all, my Daddy knew a lot of important people. Besides, I had always known in my heart that Daddy was on speaking terms with jolly old Saint Nick.

Throughout our lives, there are those extraordinary, once-in-a-life-time events that remain engraved in our hearts and minds forever. For me, one of those moments is the day I received my first hug and kiss from the gentle giant who spoke with a thick Dutch accent. For Richard and me, and the entire Magney household, Eric was to become our best friend, substitute father, the representation of all that is love, patience, forgiveness and understanding. Eric would become our intimate confidant. The memory of Eric and Erna Bert van Werald was to be etched in our minds for all time.

KAREN AND KAY

I can't remember if it was the first summer or the second summer that we had been in our home on 22nd Street, but I do know that I was no older than six.

My cousin Karen—Aunt Ginny's daughter—had come to stay with us for a couple of weeks. Aunt Ginny was Mom's younger sister, Virginia. As a little child, I could not pronounce the word Virginia, but I did create my own special name for my favorite, and dearly loved, aunt. At first I referred to her as Gina, and eventually Gina became Ginny.

Karen was Aunt Ginny's oldest child – three and a half years older than I. Even though we were cousins and there was an age difference of three years, Karen has always seemed like my older sister. In my eyes, Karen was perfect and beautiful. Like most members of the Schafer family, she was long and lanky, blond, with brown eyes, had thick dark eyebrows and the most perfect set of pearly white teeth. She was blessed with a Hollywood like smile to match that perfect set of teeth!

From the time Mom and Dad moved back to Spokane, Karen and I have been inseparable. During the holidays and school breaks, we would take turns staying at each other's homes. She was always very protective of me, watching over me like a mother hen, had enduring patience with me, and basically was the one who taught me about "the birds and the bees." In reality, however, my behavior at times was more like that of a bratty kid sister, instead of an adoring younger sibling.

Our next door neighbors, the first two years we lived in our new home, were Don and Catherine Morton and family. They had two daughters,

Monica, who was about thirteen, and Kay, who was about ten. They had an adorable springer spaniel named Molly.

Monica was always carrying a load of books with her and trying to be serious and sophisticated. Kay, on the other hand, was the younger kid sister who could have cared less about her sister's sophistication.

Kay's face was full of freckles, and I thought that was a terrific facial feature. She had brown hair, usually in pigtails. The Mortons, like many of the families who lived on 22nd Street, were devoted Catholics who went to church at St. Augustine's Parish. Monica and Kay attended the parish schools and always wore uniforms. The girls did not like them at all!

Karen and Kay became good friends and enjoyed playing with each whenever they could. They would take turns playing at each others homes. I recall those two playing beauty shop, dress up, and going off on their own to play with each other and I was not included. Mom always wanted me to play with my younger brother Richard. Mom felt Karen needed to have some time away from me. I, on the other hand, believed I should be Karen's constant shadow and companion.

One particular summer day, temperatures had been consistently in the 90's for what seemed like forever, and the evening temps in the 70's. Mid-morning Mom decided to take us kids to Comstock park to go swimming and play on the swings and slide for a couple of hours. When we returned home, Mom prepared a delicious lunch that consisted of sandwiches, potato chips and the most refreshing sugary beverage, Kool Aid.

Following lunch, Karen asked if Kay could stay and play in the back yard. The two girls were planning to play beauty shop. Mom approved and set up a couple of TV trays for them, along with a card table for curlers and brushes and combs.

I assumed, of course, that I would be a part of the beauty shop and be with Karen and Kay. Mom, however, felt I should take a nap because I had been "playing hard in the heat!" This was a favorite saying of Mom's when she wanted us to take a nap. I couldn't believe it! No way was I going to take a nap when the others were playing beauty shop. I was so outraged that I knocked over the TV trays and the card table and spilled the supplies all over the yard.

I was, in other words, a most obnoxious brat!

When Mom called for me to come in the house, I refused to listen to her and ignored her tone of voice, pretending I didn't hear her. Little did I realize that my mother had very quietly come out of the house and was standing beside me. But smarty me, continued to ignore her instructions. Before I knew it, she grabbed one of my arms and with one of her arms, swung a belt that produced a quick and throbbing sting to my legs.

I was immediately marched inside and put to bed for the remainder of the afternoon.

By today's standard for raising children, this type of discipline would not be acceptable. This, however, was how my mother was raised as a child and this was how she raised her children. If you "spare the rod you will spoil the child." Spoiled, bratty children were not to be part of the Magney household. As a youngster, I was strong-willed and determined to have my way. My mother, fortunately, was a strong willed parent who was trying her best to teach her head-strong daughter how to be respectful and obedient.

Speaking of my naughty behavior, I remember another incident involving Karen when I let my temper get the better of me. Once again, Mom was granting what I considered a special privilege to Karen. For whatever reason, I had to remain inside the house and was not allowed to go with Karen and Kay. I became so enraged I grabbed a long sharp butcher knife from the kitchen counter and started chasing Karen around the dining room table.

Karen began screaming for Mom. When Mom saw what I was doing, she immediately went for Dad's famous belt. Once again I felt the sting and throbbing pain on my legs. Mother was an expert at swinging that belt! Needless to say, I spent the rest of the day in my room convinced that I was being abused, while Karen, who never did anything wrong, went off and had a grand time with her best friend, Kay Morton.

Many times through the years, Karen and I have reminisced about the butcher knife incident. When we do, it is with laughter and fond memories of sister-like moments that we shared with each other.

A Side Note.

I must mention that whenever I behaved like a spoiled brat, it was always Karen who was there to console me with words of sisterly wisdom and love. She always saw the funny side of what I had done and was most forgiving. Now, so many years later, I can truly say it is Karen who has been a source of strength and inspiration for me. She has lifted me up when I was down. She has always been the first to praise me when I exceeded my goals and accomplishments in life.

THE NIX FAMILY

When I was four years old, I was introduced to Shirley Nix at First Presbyterian Church. Little did I know or realize that we would develop a life long friendship that would see us through fun times and difficult moments.

Our friendship really began when we started kindergarten at Roosevelt Grade School. Mom was very concerned that I have someone to walk to school with every day. Shirley's mother, Mona Nix, and my mother were good friends and belonged to the same church circle known as Lucia Pratt. The Nix family actually lived two blocks away from us on 24th.

Mona and Mom had lived fairly similar lives. Like Mona, Mom had been exposed to country living in Clayton, Washington, where Grandma's older sister, Aunt Etta, and Uncle Ernest had a small farm. It was there Mom would ride horses and spend her summers helping feed the work hands who assisted with the harvest. When she graduated from North Central High School, Mom took a job working at Peters and Sons Florist. She answered the phone and took orders from the floral customers. Her job, however, was short term. As soon as she acquired enough skills, she went to work as a receptionist for Dr. Elizabeth White.

Mona was three months older than Mom. She was born in Midland, South Dakota and attended the Midland Schools for 11 of the 12 years. Mona's mother taught piano lessons and her father was a postal carrier. Other close family members lived on a ranch near by.

The depression years were tough for Mona's family in South Dakota. Her dad lost his job with the post office and the extended family lost the family ranch. This meant Mona had to give up her dearly loved horse and all of her friends to move to Rapid City, South Dakota. Shortly after these hardships occurred, her brother, Roy, her parents, grandfather and great aunt moved to Spokane. Mona's father had the good fortune to land a postal job as a mail carrier. Mona graduated from high school in Rapid City and then attended Kinman Business University in Spokane. She then went to work for Peters & Sons Florist as a book-keeper. Like most young women and like my Mom, Mona lived at home with her parents.

Bob Nix, Shirley's father, was born in Anamoose, North Dakota in 1913. He grew up an only child. His father was a pharmacist and worked all over Montana going from job to job while Bob was a youngster. His family eventually settled in Great Falls, Montana, where he graduated from high school. In 1937, following the death of his mother, he moved to Spokane.

Bob and Mona met in January 1941. Bob and his roommate shared an apartment on South Monroe near 5th. The guys decided it would be fun to double date one evening. Bob's roommate already had a special girlfriend, and Bob asked his roommate if she might have a special friend. By gosh, she did have such a friend, her name was Mona Howes. Mona lived on the north side of the Spokane River on Howard and Indiana. Mona was tall and thin with beautiful dark blonde hair and big blue eyes.

Bob's roommate introduced Bob to Mona Howes and the rest is history. Six months later, on July 3, 1941, they were married in the home of Mona's parents.

Bob was working at the Kress Five & Dime store on Main Street. In the 40s and the 50s, all businesses closed their doors for the major holiday celebrations. The Fourth of July was one of the most important and highly celebrated holidays for the entire country. By being married on the third of July, Bob and Mona had an extra day to celebrate their marriage before Bob had to return to work.

Like all young men in the early 40's Bob tried to enlist in the military. Bob, however, had been rejected by the armed services for active duty because he was "too skinny." After being denied by the military, he decided to attend an on-the-job training program at the Spokane Army Air Depot in October of 1942. His training enabled him to eventually become a junior engineering draftsman.

In order to save money for a down payment on a home, Bob and Mona decided to live with her parents who owned a home on Howard and Indiana. While living with Mona's parents and attending classes at the air depot, Bob made a career change and took a good paying job at the Post Movie Theater operating the movie projectors.

During the few years that the Nixes lived with Mona's parents, two daughters, Tana and Shirley, were born. It was becoming apparent the home on Indiana was quickly becoming too small for this family of four. Shirley was almost two when Mona learned she was once again expecting baby number three, another girl to be named Donna.

Bob wanted to use the skills he had developed in drafting. Now with the thought of another little mouth to feed, a decision was made to build a new home. In 1947 they found the perfect lot on the South Hill to build their little castle in the sky.

The Nix house on 24th was designed and built by Bob. The project took Bob more than a year to complete. He worked on the construction of the brick bungalow home on the weekends and in the evenings. The skills that he learned from the training program enabled Bob to draw the plans for their new home. Bob and Mona, with Shirley and her older sister Tana Jean, moved into the brick bungalow home in fall of 1948. Donna was born in December. The home had two bedrooms and one bath room on the first floor. The kitchen by today's standards would have been small and cramped, but was very ample for a home built in 1948. The basement was mostly unfinished. Bob, however, realizing that he had a young growing family, designed space in the basement for future bedrooms. Their one car garage was unattached to the house and actually sat towards the back of the house.

Bob and Mona Nix were members of First Presbyterian Church by the time my mom and dad moved back to Spokane in 1947. Mona belonged to the same women's organization that Mom joined. While Bob did not sing in the church choir, he loved music and enjoyed listening to the choir and my father's deep bass voice.

Shortly after Mom and Dad moved into our slate green cedar-shake house at 205 W- 22nd Street, Mom approached Mona and asked her if Shirley and

Tana would stop by the house and walk to school with me.

Roosevelt Grade School was located on 14th and Bernard. This section of the South Hill was a main thoroughfare for traffic heading downtown or to the north side of Spokane. The school was a mile away from our home. Mom's concern for my safety was justified by the fact that there was a lot of traffic on Bernard Street, plus, a section of Manito Park that was located on Bernard Street from 21st to 19th. This part of the park looked like blocks of vacant lots, with trees, dried grasses and wild flowerers.

Many parents would have driven their children to school if they lived a mile away from home, but Mom did not have a driver's license and was almost paranoid about getting one, so I walked to and from school every day.

A SIDE NOTE.

In 1951, most of the city schools did not have busses to transport their students to and from school, unless it was to athletic games. When Shirley and I started kindergarten, Spokane had a population of almost one hundred thousand, crime was not a problem and child abductions were unheard of in the community. It was a common practice for young children to walk a mile to school, unaccompanied by a parent, as long as they were walking in groups of three or four.

At the time my mother approached Mona with the request for me to walk to school with her girls, neither mother, or Shirley and I for that matter, realized the close ties that would be knit together by two little girls walking to and from school. Fifty-three years later we remain the best of friends.

The Bob and Mona Nix family in 1959. Shirley is standing next to her father, Bob. In the front row, left to right is Tim, Chris, Donna, Tana and Mona Nix.

FAVORITE THEATERS IN SPOKANE

Spokane housed a number of movie theaters. For a community with a population of not more than one hundred thousand people in the early fifties, it was amazing to see so many theaters in the city. These buildings did serve many purposes in the early years of Spokane's history. The theaters provided the community with live plays, motion pictures and musical concerts. The movie theaters were virtually the heart of the city's entertainment district.

Mom and Dad were great fans of the arts, and enjoyed attending live theater, motion pictures and the symphony. As parents, they believed it was part of a child's proper upbringing and educational experience to be exposed to all three.

As kids, we referred to the movies as going to a "show." When we went to see live stage presentations, we referred to this experience as "going to the theater." When attending the Spokane Symphony, we said we were going to the "Symphony," but for other musical events we were going to "a concert."

There were several theaters that have fond memories for me. One of the most elaborate was the Fox Theater, which was part of a chain of theaters. This chain also owned the State, Orpheum, and Liberty theaters. Of these theaters, The Fox Theater to me was electrifying. The walls contained art deco designs with eagles, turtles, plants and sunbursts that decorated each side of the stage. The ceilings were high and immense. I always imagined this theater to be as grand as the theaters in Hollywood. When attending a movie, I would pretend that I would see one of the Hollywood celebrities waltzing down the long staircase waving at the crowd of spectators. At this theater, the usherettes or ushers wore spiffy uniforms that looked like they were tailor-made for each employee.

Another favorite was the Post Street Theater, located near Post and Trent, which is now known as Spokane Falls Boulevard. The lobby of this theater was of marble and mahogany. The theater was fairly large and had a seating capacity for almost 1500 people. As I remember, the interior of the theater had ornate plaster ceilings and wall decorations that incorporated numerous scrolls and floral patterns. Large plaster columns stood on each side of the stage. There were engravings of smiling faces, and bunches of grapes or flowers.

The stage was very large, which made it suitable for all kinds of theatrical productions. Mom and Dad, along with Eric and Erna Bert, used to attend the Spokane Symphony concerts at this splendid theater. I was given the fun privilege of accompanying my parents along with Eric and Erna Bert to Symphony concerts at The Post Theater.

There was a very special reason why I preferred the Post Theater to all the others in downtown Spokane. My best friend's father worked at this theater as one of the movie projectionists. If Bob Nix knew we were in the audience, he would flash a welcome sign on the screen "Welcome Jack and Dorothy to The Post Theater, or Welcome Marilyn to the Post Theater." Of course, this always made us feel like celebrities. I guess you could say I have always felt a special connection to the Post Theater due to Bob Nix and my dear friend Shirley.

When the Post Theater closed in the seventies, Bob went to work at The Garland Theater on North Monroe and Garland. The Garland Theater, which was built in 1945, was the first in Spokane to have its own adjacent parking lot. It was also the first theater to be built away from the downtown core of the city.

THONGS INVENTED BY SHIRLEY

I have heard it said that the best and most creative inventors throughout time and history are children.

Children have the best imaginations and when put to the task, can write the best stories, design the tallest buildings and create the most imaginative board games and card games.

Children aren't concerned with the simple fact that someone years before tried to invent the very same article but did not succeed. Nor do they take into consideration that this invention might be too costly to produce or that their new little idea is totally useless.

I know this for a fact. When Shirley and I were seven years old she came up with the most creative and practical invention I had ever seen. At the time that she put her talents and mind to work on her designer skills, we had recently completed the second grade. One day during our summer vacation, Shirley walked down to my house so we could play together. We wanted something creative to do, so Shirley told me about an idea she had for "Summer Shoes."

Shirley loved going barefoot more than anything. Due to the blistery heat of a hot summer day, where the sidewalks and streets become like fiery furnaces, it was not wise to be without a pair of shoes.

On this particular August day, the weather had been dry and sizzling with heat. Both Shirley and I were wearing shorts and sleeveless shirts (commonly referred to in the fifties as "crop tops"), trying to stay as cool as possible.

I did enjoy going bare foot on a hot summer day and wiggling my tender toes in the thick, lush, green grass of our yard. However, our slate green, one story home on 22nd Street, had a large front yard and an even bigger back yard. with a humongous vacant lot that sat on the east side of the house. On this lot were the tallest Ponderosa Pine trees imaginable, and in these trees were a zillion bees' nests. It only took a couple of times to realize going bare foot in the summer meant I would end up with swollen feet from numerous bee stings. Unfortunately, I had learned from the school of hard knocks that I was better off wearing a pair of sweaty canvas shoes on a hot summer day than to feel the pain inflicted by those darn old bees.

Shirley, however, was much braver and stronger willed than I was. Bees in the grass and scorching side walk pavement didn't prevent her from running barefoot.

Shirley and I were as opposite as two little girls could be. I was always envious of Shirley because I was very short and tiny with thin, straight dark auburn hair and green eyes. Shirley was built like her parents, tall, thin and stately. In fact, as a youngster, Shirley was so thin that at times she looked like a pin that might snap in half if it wasn't held just right. Her arms and legs, simply put, were long and skinny. She was blessed with the most beautiful face, and a gorgeous head of thick, blonde curly hair. Like all the members of her family, she had piercing blue eyes that looked like the sky, rosy red cheeks and when she would smile, the prettiest dimples would form in her cheeks.

To me, Shirley was the prettiest and sweetest person in the whole wide world, next to Karen.

Even though physically, Shirley and I have always looked like "Mutt and Jeff," we had personalities that were much the same, and therefore a compliment to one another.

We could talk for hours. She was an excellent listener and had the softest voice. Shirley was very athletic and was very smart in school. I was neither of those things. Both of us, however, were rather shy and quiet girls. We would rather sit in the back of the room and try not be noticed by the teacher.

Much to our delight, school was closed for summer vacation. We made it a point to play together at least once a week. On this one particular hot summer afternoon in mid August, we found ourselves bored, and wanting something different to do. We decided to embark on her stunning idea for creating "Summer Shoes." This truly would be a new concept in foot wear that would benefit both of our feet, Shirley was going to begin the task by creating a pair of shoes that could be worn on a hot summer day, protect the soles of feet from hot cement, and allow the feet to remain cool. This new shoe design, however, would be especially beneficial for me. The new summer shoe would enable me to walk on the grass in our back yard. I would not have to worry about getting stung by another bee. These summer sandals would be the perfect summer shoe for any person. The foot could remain cool because there would be no leather or material surrounding the foot. The bottom of the shoe would be made of leather. However, for our initial design purposes, we would start with reliable, and easy to come by, *cardboard*.

I can see it as if it were yesterday. Shirley, with crayon in hand, put her feet on the cardboard and traced the outline of her feet. I stood on another piece of card board with bare feet. Once again, with crayon in hand, she traced the outline of my two feet. The next step was to cut out the outline of our two feet with scissors. This took a while because it was difficult for our little fingers to manipulate the scissors on stiff cardboard. As I recall we took turns helping one another with this skill because our small fingers became sore. The tracing of the foot was easy, but the cutting of the card board was another matter. It took most of our time that afternoon. At last, we had two sets of feet. It was very easy to tell whose set of cardboard feet belonged to whom. Shirley's were long and skinny and looked more oblong in length. My foot prints resembled a short, fat, square box.

The next phase of this important invention would call for strong and sturdy string. Shirley put her feet on the card board outlines and had me take a crayon and place it in between her large toe and the second toe. With the crayon, I was to make a make a round mark on the card board foot print. She then had me stand on my foot prints and she took the crayon and made the same mark on the cardboard. Shirley's inventive mind knew we would be poking a hole through that mark so we could place our string loop through this hole.

The first time our string was too short, and the next time we had too much. After we decided on the correct amount of string for these new shoes, Shirley realized she would need strong tape. She had to firmly tape both ends of the string loop to the sole of the shoe. After that chore was accomplished, she had to insert the string loop through the hole, and this was slipped over one toe, in order to hold the toe to the shoe. With another piece of string, the same idea was used at the ankle.

By the end of the afternoon we had created our very first and most fashionable pair of thong shoes. Now for the first time in my life, I could walk out into my own back yard without the fear of stepping on another bee and getting stung.

As the hot afternoon came to end and Shirley's mother wanted her to come home for dinner, Shirley's creative energies came to fruition. I have colorful memories of Shirley proudly putting on her new designer thongs and clomp, clomp, clomped throughout our house, going up and down the basement steps for practice. Picking up each foot and putting it down as if pulling a foot out of thick mud because this was the only way we could walk in the "Summer Shoes" and keep them on our feet. As she departed, I can vividly see the big grin that was on her face, her wavy blonde hair flying in the summer breeze and hear the flip-flop, flip-flop, of the card board thongs clomping on the sidewalk pavement.

My best friend and I had just invented the most valuable pair of summer shoes I would ever wear, The Thong! Thanks to Shirley, I did not suffer another bee sting on the bottom of my foot for the remainder of that summer.

Today, Shirley's "Summer Shoe" is the most popular and sought after shoe in the world. If only we had known what it meant to PATENT!

THE EUGENE FAMILY

Life in our new house had been grand. The first year went by so quickly. The Morton family-Don, Catherine, Monica, and Kay and their Springer spaniel Molly, were loved by everyone on the block. It was wonderful to be spoiled by folks who lived next door. It was early summer. I had just completed first grade and cousin Karen came to stay with us for a couple of weeks.

Karen and Kay Morton had developed a nice friendship; both were the same age and both had the same interests. During dinner one evening, Karen made the statement to us that "she was going to miss her new friend, Kay."

I asked her why? Karen stated, "They are selling the house and moving away."

At first, I didn't believe Karen, and asked Mom if this was so. She said, "Yes! Mr. Morton is being transferred by the company he works for, and the whole family will be moving to a new city. We will be having new next door neighbors."

My heart sank! I didn't want new neighbors. I liked the ones we had.

Moving day, however, eventually arrived and the Morton family bid their farewells to friends and neighbors on 22nd Street. About a week after seeing one moving truck pull away from the house, another one arrived.

I was most hopeful that our new neighbors would have a daughter about my age. My hopes soon faded when I learned they had a son, Michael who was Richard's age, and a little girl who was two and a half years old named Celia. I certainly thought this was unfair. Karen had Kay to play with, Richard would now have Mike to play with and, once again, I would have no one.

Why couldn't Celia be my age? Life wasn't fair, or so I thought.

Our new next door neighbors were Dick and Joan Eugene. While listening to Mom and Dad talk, I did learn that Mr. Eugene had briefly dated Daddy's young sister, Mary Anne, many years back. The Eugenes, like the Morton family, were a strong Catholic family and members of St. Augustine's Parish on Bernard and 18th.

Within the first month after the Eugenes occupied the old Morton home, I was perplexed with an unusual observation I had made about this family. Michael and Celia's father, Dick Eugene, drove a rather odd and unusual vehicle to and from work every day. He didn't drive a car like my daddy. His car was like a huge station wagon or a truck with a top on it. The vehicle was painted a dark green color and had big yellow letters printed on both sides. The vehicle did not look like a pick-up, nor did it resemble the ever so popular station wagon of the 50s. It did, however, resemble the modern day mini van that had become popular with families in the 80s. What Dick Eugene was driving to and from work was the company's floral delivery truck. There were two doors on the back of the truck and whenever Mr. Eugene opened the doors, flowers could be seen neatly arranged in boxes. At other times, there would be enormous arrangements of flowers that were in giant white baskets. What I remember most about this delivery truck was the wonderful floral aroma that would soar through the air.

Little did I know or realize that the Eugene family owned one of the nicest and most prestigious flower shops (Eugene's Flowers) in Spokane.

Dick and Joan operated the business with Dick's father, E.S. Eugene Sr. E.S. Sr. was actually the founder of this very successful enterprise.

Mr. E.S. Eugene, Sr. was born in Poland. His parents died at an early age. He went to live with an aunt when he was eight. When he was fourteen, he left his aunt's house and went to Budapest and worked for a florist family. In Europe in the early 1900s, business men would take young men into their business and train them, while providing them with room and board.

Several years later, Mr. Eugene went to Berlin where he obtained a job with a florist. He traveled throughout Europe winning prizes for his artistic floral displays. One day while reading the newspapers, he began to realize that war was coming and Germany would be involved. It was at that point he thought about leaving Europe. He moved to America in 1905. E.S. was 21 years old when he arrived in America and took a job at a large flower shop in St. Louis.

He loved his work, and the people he met, but he missed a very dear lady friend who had taken a position as housekeeper for a wealthy family in Berlin. Numerous months passed before E.S. decided to return to Berlin and ask this wonderful lady if she would consider living in America, and marrying him.

The young couple returned to America, living in St. Louis for several years. The weather in St. Louis was hot and sultry. Mosquitoes were a continual problem because St. Louis sits on the Mississippi River. While reading the newspaper one day, he saw an ad seeking a florist manager in Spokane, Washington. E.S. responded to the ad.

Mr. Eugene accepted the job, and he and his wife left St. Louis. He found the work with the Spokane florist challenging and rewarding, but deep in his heart, his dream was to have his own business. The first Eugene's Flower Shop opened its doors in downtown Spokane on April 30, 1908.

Mr. and Mrs. Eugene had several children. Their oldest son carried the nick name of Dick, but his given name was E.S., Jr.

Dick and his wife, Joan, were destined to carry on the family dream, as they supplied Spokane residents with elegant floral arrangements. They designed arrangements for weddings, funerals, civic events, church sanctuaries, and for all sorts of private parties.

Knowing that these new neighbors were in the floral business, made my mother jubilant. She loved to grow flowers and decorate with them. More exciting for the Magney family was the opportunity for Grandpa Schafer to converse with someone in German. Because Grandpa loved flowers and was very involved with the Spokane Rose Society, had started the Orchid Society, he had personally known ES., Sr. When grandpa was semi-retired, he built a green house in his back yard so he could enjoy his gardening hobby throughout the entire year. Having the Eugenes as neighbors would afford Grandpa Schafer the chance to share his love of flowers and gardening.

My younger brother Richard also lucked out because he had a new play-mate, Michael. Because Mom and Dad were close in age to Dick and Joan Eugene, new friendships were quickly made, and the Magney family couldn't have been happier.

Several months after Mom and Dad had brought new baby sister Janice, home from the hospital, Mom announced the Eugenes also had a new baby. We were going to go over to their house to welcome the new baby. I thought this was very strange, and questioned if Mom knew what she was talking about. She must have gotten her facts mixed up. Joan Eugene did not get fat like Mom, so how could she have a baby. It was then I learned about the word *adoption*. Joan and Dick had just adopted a little baby girl and named her Patti. Patti and Janice were born just a few months apart. The word was out that 22nd Street had two new baby girls! Hallelujah!

This was exciting to everyone but me. I was patiently waiting for God to answer my request for a friend my age to move on to 22nd street. At the age of seven, I found it very easy to have a pity party for myself.

The best memories that I have of Joan Eugene are two-fold. I loved listening to her practice her singing with two other ladies. Joan had a voice that sounded like a song bird. Music and singing were her passion. One of the ladies in the trio was Mrs. Rodkey, a family friend and choir member at First Presbyterian Church. These ladies could make beautiful harmony, and were frequently invited to entertain at various clubs and civic events in Spokane.

Joan's other wonderful quality was her laugh. She loved to laugh and smile, and seemed to find humor in almost any situation. In all the years that I have known this sweet Christian lady, I have never heard her say an unkind word about anyone. I have also never seen her lose her temper, raise her voice, or get angry.

Joan was born and raised in Kansas City, Missouri. While in high school, she worked at the Kress store after school and on the weekends. Following high school graduation, she attended St. Teresa's for one year. Joan studied music and took private voice lessons on Saturdays. To help pay for her tuition, she worked with a Girl Scout Group and at Metropolitan Life Insurance Company. Following the one year at St. Teresa's, she took some business classes at Huff's Business College.

One summer Joan went to Chicago to visit a good friend. Here she learned that salaries in Chicago were much better than in Kansas City. So, on a whim, she responded to an ad in the newspaper for a position at a furniture store.

She landed the job at the Merchandise Mart and soon learned that she was working at the largest furniture store in the world, and earning $100 a month.

Chicago was becoming a very busy and important mid western city. The war in Europe and with Japan was heating up. There were thousands of soldiers and sailors training and shipping out for the Great Lakes Naval Station.

While living in this big windy city, Joan managed to attend the theater and the opera. She also enjoyed attending live radio broadcasts, especially when Don Ameche was appearing as a guest.

Joan's good friend, Helen, joined the Navy and encouraged Joan to enlist. At first, Joan said 'no,' as she was not interested.

While working at the Merchandise Mart, Joan became aware that Washington D.C. had sent thousands of its federal employees to Chicago to live and work. At that time in the nation's history, there was great fear that Washington D.C. would be bombed.

One day Joan walked into a Navy recruiting station and joined the WAVES. She decided she wanted to support her country and see the world. Many of her closest friends were serving in the military.

Joan was first sent to New York for boot camp, and then to New Orleans, to work in the Federal Building. She wrote the orders for the ships going to the Pacific via the Panama Canal. She also wrote orders for all the newly constructed ships coming down the Mississippi River headed for the Gulf of Mexico. These ships met ships coming down the Eastern Seaboard to form convoys for the troop ships heading for the Pacific Theater of Operations.

Joan had been in New Orleans only a short time. She hardly had a chance to get use to her new uniform, when one evening, she and four other WAVES decided to have dinner at a nice hotel. While eating, four handsome young soldiers came to their table and introduced themselves. They were from Robbins Field in Mobile, Alabama. Like all young single people during the war years, it was easy to strike up a conversation with strangers and quickly make friends. The table of four soon became a table of eight.

Following dinner, a tall lanky young Sergeant escorted her out of the hotel and asked if he could take her to Sunday Mass at St. Louis Cathedral. Joan accepted the invitation. After Mass, they enjoyed a leisurely lunch until Tech Sergeant E.S. (Dick) Eugene had to board a train to head back to Mobile. His three day pass was soon to expire.

That week, Sergeant Eugene was successful in securing another weekend pass for New Orleans. As soon as he arrived in the seaport city, he called Joan to ask if he could take her to Mass and out to lunch. While eating lunch, Dick mentioned that he grew up in Spokane, Washington. Joan, somewhat embarrassed, admitted she had never heard of the place. After saying good night to Dick, she immediately went searching for her atlas to locate the city of Spokane.

As their friendship continued to grow, it became apparent that the two were falling in love. At Christmas, Joan and Dick managed to get holiday passes. They traveled by train to Kansas City, so Dick could meet Joan's parents. On Christmas Eve before Midnight Mass, E.S. Dick Eugene asked Joan to marry him (after the war!)

At the conclusion of a joyful holiday celebration with Joan's family, the young engaged couple headed back to their respective jobs.

As happened so often when couples were surrounded by the pressures of

Playing football in the Magney's back yard
Left to right: Celia Eugene, Karina Zilgme, Marilyn Magney, Richard Magney, Jim Allers and Mike Eugene.

Patti Eugene and Janice Magney sitting on the front porch of the Magney house with their favorite tricycle.

war, their engagement was very short, lasting only six weeks. They decided to get married at the St. Louis Cathedral when Dick learned he was receiving orders to go overseas. They asked each other the questions so many other couples were asking each other—why wait?

Within a few weeks, he received word that his unit was scheduled to be sent to the South Pacific in August. As soon as he received definite orders, both applied for a brief leave so they could make a quick trip to Spokane to be with Dick's family before he was shipped overseas.

Tech Sergeant Eugene spent two years in the South Pacific. During that time, he sent Joan over 200 letters.

At the end of World War II, Joan left the Navy and moved to California to be with her parents and brothers, while waiting for her husband to return from home.

Tech Sergeant Eugene, like so many of the hundreds of young Spokanites returning to his home town following the war, was anxious to put the war behind him and begin a new life with his wife. Dick's aging parents badly needed his help with the family's rapidly expanding floral business. Consequently, Dick and Joan did not have to look for work. Work came to them. Joan used her education in business to manage the ordering, the accounts receivable and payable, and set delivery schedules. Dick was blessed with his father's artistic talents for arranging breathtaking floral bouquets. Both Dick and his father filled in as delivery men, and would often be seen setting up baskets for weddings and funeral services.

As a couple, Dick and Joan Eugene worked side by side to grow and develop the family business, raise their three children and support their parish. Their love for people and God, along with their generous yet gentle personalities, set a special example in the eyes of everyone. Every two years, they traded in the old floral van for a new, more modern and efficient vehicle. As I aged, I began to realize their unusual looking truck would some day become the fore runner of the very popular delivery and mini vans of the 80s.

SEVERAL SIDE NOTES.

It is with great sadness that, as I write this book, Patti has called me to tell me that her brother Michael has just passed away. He died at Sacred Heart Hospital, in April 2004, from complications with diabetes.

Michael is the first of our gang from 22nd Street to leave this world.

Michael was born January 30, 1947. In the 1970s he attended the Chicago School of Art. He lived in Detroit for many years. He was well known for his art displays which were featured in numerous art galleries throughout Michigan. For those of us who grew up with Mike, we were not the least surprised to learn he was a well known artist and had made a name for himself. Even as a child, he was gifted and creative.

At the time of Mike's death, he had been living in Elk, Washington with his wife, Daphne. Today, Mike's only child, Sean, is about 35 years old and like his father is an aspiring artist living in San Antonio, Texas. On behalf of everyone who lived on 22nd Street, it is with deep sorrow and a heavy heart that we say goodbye to our dear friend Michael Eugene.

During their growing up years, Janice and Patti remained the very best of friends. They shared their hopes, dreams and secrets with one another. They supported and prayed for one another through those difficult adolescent years when we sometimes find new friends and leave the old ones behind. Now in their early fifties, they remain close pals, even though distance separates them.

Today, Patti is a grandmother and lives in Spokane, with her husband, Lynn. They have two grown daughters.

Janice lives in Bonney Lake, Washington. She has two handsome sons. Eric, the older, is a deputy sheriff with the King County Sheriff's Department. Her younger son Adam, is in the Army, has recently served in Afghanistan for a year with the 100th Airborne Division, and more recently a year in Iraq with the Stryker Brigade from Fort Lewis.

In later years, when the Eugenes sold their home and moved out by Whitworth, Dorothy and Joan remained close friends and continued their friendship by telephone and yearly get-togethers.

Little did I realize when I first met the Eugene family that both my Janice and her best friend Patti (seven years my junior) would have a life long loving impact on my life.

As for Patti and myself, God granted us the ability to nurture a long time friendship and remain in close contact with one another. Little Patti Eugene will always be my sister in Christ.

LILAC FESTIVAL TIME IN SPOKANE

The Flower Festival Parade was the forerunner of the Lilac Festival. Early settlers brought lilac shoots with them on the long journey across country, planting them here in their new home. Lilacs were known as the friendship flower. Today, especially in older parts of Spokane, lilac trees bend over clapboard houses and can be seen gracing new homes and office buildings throughout the city. During the month of May, the air is filled with the scent of these favorite old fashioned blooms.

Spokane's first Lilac Festival grew from the Flower Festival. It began May 17, 1938, and continued until the 24th. The parade consisted of seven decorated automobiles and eight school girls throwing sprigs of lilacs to onlookers from a float. The focus was truly on the beautiful lilacs. Following the parade, a flower show was sponsored by the Associated Garden Clubs.

As a child, I remember during the Lilac Festival Mom used to recall a story about her former boss, Dr. Elizabeth White, who won the blue ribbon sweepstakes in 1938 for her lilac specimens.

In 1939 the parade had one float. That year the American Legion drill team presented lilacs to passengers on arriving trains and busses. The first Lilac Queen was in 1940. Through all of the '40s and until 1958, the contest was open only to women 18 years and older. High School bands first participated in the parade in 1940. In 1942, the first coronation ball was held and crowned Bobbee Judd Eddy as its third Lilac queen. During the war years, the Lilac Festival was discontinued, but in 1945 the festival resumed, and the Lilac Festival Association was born. The Association members decided to focus on having a beautiful parade and lilac show, decorating the city, and holding a contest for a queen. By 1948, the parade had 40 bands and 30 floats.

The Lilac Festival in the 1940s was a far cry from the sophisticated, smooth-running festival and parade of today. But what it lacked in polish, it made up for in excitement and community support. Today, sheer numbers demand that there be standards and guidelines which somewhat determine the scope of the parade floats, as well as limit participation in the various events.

Initially, there was only one parade and this was on the third Saturday of the month of May. In the mid 50s, the Armed Forces Day Parade and the Lilac Parade merged. Daddy was so proud of this that he used to show me an old photograph taken in 1937 of the 161st Regiment of the Washington National Guard. The picture showed soldiers on an army truck with rifles, barbed wire and bags. The sign on the army truck read, "Enlist in 161st Regiment – Drills on Monday, Tuesday." Dad felt a historical moment had been reached in Spokane when the two parades became the Lilac Festival/Armed Forces Day Parade on Saturday mornings. Later a Thursday night Torchlight Parade was established in 1960, and eventually surpassed the Saturday morning parade in popularity. Then in 1976, the two parades were merged into the on Lilac Festival/Armed Forces Torchlight Parade.

Professional, and civic and community groups were encouraged to enter a float in the Saturday morning parade. A long time member of what was, in 1944, the Spokane Chapter of the National Secretaries Association, remembers being a part of the float committee. "Everyone participated. Together we designed the float, bent the chicken wire and for hours and hours and hours, we made tissue paper flowers to fit into that chicken wire frame that was placed around the car. The night before the parade, some 15 or 16 of us volunteered to spend the last hours preparing for the early dawn drive to the head of the parade. Usually, Spokane's Secretary of the Year, chosen by the organization for her professional skills, rode on the float."

Entries in the Lilac Festival parade, in the '40s and '50s, included professionally done floats and those that were not done professionally, along with

1953 Lilac Festival parade featuring a float sponsored by the Crescent Department Store

school bands, individual children entries of wagons, bikes, dogs and cats. Big favorites were the horses from the various 4-H clubs and Sheriff's Posse. Throughout the parade would be clowns galore, all throwing candy to the spectators. The candy throwing, in recent years, has also gone by the wayside in the interest of safety of both participants and viewers.

I am not sure how old I was when I attended my first Lilac Parade. I do know that, as a child, I missed very few parades, as Dad was very involved with the planning.

For my family, the excitement began on Friday night with a large festival and program at the Joe Albi Stadium. Famous entertainers such as Hop-Along Cassidy, Ed Sullivan, Spike Jones, Gordon McRae, the Ink Spots, Peggy Lee and Jimmy Rodgers were just a few of the entertainers brought to the Lilac City to entertain the crowds of people. In addition, there would be circus acts, jugglers, military bands, and, of course, military armor leading the dignitaries onto the field. Then, on Saturday morning at 10 am, the bomber planes from Fairchild Air Force Base would officially start the parade by flying low over the city making their deafening noise.

Because Daddy played a prominent role with the National Guard, he was very involved with the military aspect of the parade and working with the Lilac Committee. For that reason, the Magney family had choice seats for both Lilac functions on Friday night and the Saturday morning parade. In 1959, Daddy's boss, Colonel Ralph Phelps, was President of the Lilac Festival Association.

As a child, I loved the excitement that was generated in our home for the two weeks preceding the actual Lilac Festival Week. It seemed like Mom had a zillion parties to attend during that time period. She would buy a new dress for each special event. These were usually ladies' teas, some for honoring the Lilac Queen and her court, and others honoring the military dignitaries and their wives who were in town for the celebrations.

The only down side to the Lilac hoopla was the constant stream of baby sitters hired to watch over Richard, myself and Janice. Our favorite babysitter was a long time friend, Clara Hickman. Clara was a member of First Presbyterian Church. Shortly after we moved into the house, her daughter Dianna, came to live with us for a while. Diana was about fourteen at the time and attending Lewis and Clark High School. Clara was a single parent and discovered that raising a teenager presented numerous challenges. We grew attached to both Clara and Diana, and resented having any other baby sitter.

One my favorite events at the festival was the crowning of the Lilac Queen and the Grand Military Ball. This particular year the event was held at the Davenport Hotel. Like all little girls, I was in awe of the young women who represented the high schools and were vying for Lilac Queen. All little girls dream of the moment when they can wear that beautiful gown and tiara, and dance to romantic music and be waltzed around the dance floor by Prince Charming.

Because Dad and Mom would be attending the crowning of the Queen at the Military Ball, Mom approached Dad for permission to bring me to the opening ceremonies and the grand march for the dignitaries. Dad agreed, with the stipulation that Grandma and Grandpa Schafer escort me to the ball, and immediately following the crowning of the Lilac Queen, I would be taken home and put to bed.

For those who are not that familiar with the history of Spokane, The

Davenport Hotel is one of Spokane's oldest landmarks. The Hotel opened for business in 1914 and cost $3 million dollars. The Davenport Hotel was named after Louis Davenport. He owned a popular and financially lucrative restaurant. During his career he gained a reputation for being a successful entrepreneur in the hospitality business, as well as being a fair, honest and likeable gentleman.

The Davenport Hotel was a masterpiece of construction. The exterior design of the structure is old Spanish with brick and terra cotta. The eleven story building had restaurants, a lobby with fine mosaic floors and huge terra cotta pillars forming arches. These arches support a balcony 30 feet above the lobby. There were specialty shops such as the Blue Bird Shop, which sold fine china, silver and crystal. There were exclusive clothing shops for both fine gentlemen and elegant ladies. Numerous restaurants such as the men's café and a grill room in the basement provided delicious meals. With Louis Davenport's genius-level promotional campaigns, the hotel and the restaurant became internationally famous.

The hotel's opening was unique in the history of hotel operations. Louis marketing talents made him a celebrity in the eyes of fellow innkeepers.

The Spokesman-Review told about the grand opening affair. "The hundreds of guests inspecting the hotel were amazed to discover Indians in full ceremonial dress of white buckskin and feathered headdresses wandering through the public rooms. Members of the Blackfoot tribe from Glacier Park were guests of the hotel and lived in tepees which they pitched on the roof. The president of the Great Northern Railroad and a lifelong friend of Mr. Davenport brought the Indians over from the park in a special train, in honor of the opening."

Col. Charles Lindberg was one of many celebrities who stayed at the hotel during its glory days.

In 1945, Mr. Davenport sold the hotel to Mr. William Edris, president of the Olympic Hotel in Seattle.

Louis Davenport died on July 28, 1951, in his suite at the Davenport Hotel. Verus Davenport, his wife of 45 years, maintained her residence in the hotel until her death in 1967.

Jack and Dorothy Magney dancing at one of the Lilac Festival Functions in the 50's.

On the night of the Lilac Festival grand coronation ball, the lobby looked especially gorgeous. Walking through the lobby of the Davenport Hotel, I recall seeing the fountain which sat in the middle of the lobby, dressed in lilacs. The deep purples lined the base shading up to a big circle of white flowers surrounding the central figure. Every vase and jardinière was filled with beautiful lilac blossoms. The aroma that filled the air was a pure lilac fragrance. Off to one corner, an orchestra was seated. To the side of the orchestra was a lectern draped in heavy, deep purple velvet. Behind the lectern, stood the flags of the USA, and Washington State. Waiters and waitresses dressed in black and white tuxedos could be seen standing on the side, holding trays of champagne and appetizers.

The prettiest sight to see was all the elegant looking ladies who were attending this very formal event. The women were dressed in long chiffon and taffeta sleeveless gowns of every color imaginable. Their faces were adorned with brilliant, sparkling, rhinestone earrings and necklaces. Long white gloves graced the length of their arms. Women had lilacs sprinkled throughout their hair; others had very dainty, small tiaras placed on top of their heads.

The men looked as handsome and dashing as the women were beautiful. Those who were representing the military were wearing their finest dress uniforms. The civilian gentlemen could be seen wearing black tuxedos. Everyone was dressed to the hilt. Dad was dressed in his formal dress blues and looked extremely handsome. Mom looked rich and elegant in a long, full-skirted gown of chiffon that had yards of toul netting. Her dress was a deep shade of celery green which made her large green eyes look bigger and greener than ever.

I remember choking back tears as I saw Mom and Dad, the Lilac Queen and her court enter the ballroom. Each escorted on the arms of very handsome men. Violins began to play, followed by brass instruments. Speeches were made. The queen and her princesses were escorted to the dance floor, and the first waltz began. Grandma and Grandpa allowed me to see Mom and Dad dance a couple of waltzes together and then I was whisked off home to dream about the magical evening, knowing that the best was yet to come—the Big Parade!

Oh, how I loved the Saturday morning Lilac Parade. One year when I was seven and a half, Grandpa Magney was given the honors of escorting me to the Parade. Mom had given birth to Janice on April 15, and was not able to attend any of the Lilac functions that year. Dad was involved with making sure that the parade dignitaries were well taken care of. I dearly wanted to see the parade, so Dad approached Grandpa Magney and asked him if he would take me to the Parade. I am not sure who had the most fun, but I remember Grandpa clapping for all of the high school bands that marched passed us. When Lewis and Clark High School band passed, he clapped harder and said, "That's the high school your dad attended and some day when you are older you will also go to Lewis and Clark". While being awed with his enthusiasm for the school, I was more impressed with the loud up-beat rhythm of the band, the uniforms of the flag twirlers, and most of all, those large twirling flags that were bigger than the girls. In my heart I knew that some day I would be one of the fancy flag twirlers who would proudly march in front of the Lewis and Clark Band. For days following the parade, I would practice twirling a baton that Grandpa bought for me at the parade. Oh, how I loved to twirl that baton. I was getting so good at it.

I knew I wanted to take baton lessons. My baton twirling days were short lived, and I didn't get to keep the baton for very long. Mom had instructed me to only use the baton outside. I, of course, could not resist and would frequently give the baton a twirl in the living room as I was marching in the house, heading for the garage door. On one particular occasion, the baton somehow slipped out of my hand and flew through the air, landing on a cherished antique crystal vase Mom had received as a gift. The beautiful vase shattered into many pieces as I stood speechless, watching a horrific expression engulf my mothers face. My love for the baton, the dream of being a baton twirler and marching in the parade, quickly came to an end.

Grandpa Magney and I did have a fun day together that Saturday morning in May. He made me feel like I was the most special person in his life and at the parade. He introduced me to many of his friends and tenants from the Brunot Hall apartments. I was treated to all the cotton candy and hot dogs that I wanted. He bought me extra big balloons from the clowns. What more could a seven year old girl want in life—a parade and an adoring grandfather!

How fortunate I was to have a parent who played a small role in contributing to the success of this fun and exciting spring time festival for the citizens of Spokane. For me, lilac time in Spokane will always have breathtaking memories of floats, high school bands, clowns, horses and, most of all, adoring grandparents who were willing to share in the thrill of a parade. Thanks to the Associated Garden Clubs of 1938, lilacs are one of my favorite flowers. Today the Lilac/Armed Force Parade is held during the third week of May. It is still one of Spokane's most popular civic events.

SEVERAL SIDE NOTES.

In 1953 Washington State Governor, Arthur B. Langley, came to Spokane to officiate at the Lilac ceremonies, and assist with crowning the Lilac Queen. At that time in my life I did not really know who a governor was, nor what they did. By the way Mom and Dad talked about the Governor, I realized this man was a very important individual. Call it a twist of fate, or whatever you like, but little did I know that in the year 1988 I would be working for his late son, Arthur Jr., a prominent attorney in Seattle and CEO for Presbyterian Ministries Inc.

Today the Davenport Hotel has been remodeled and restored by the Worthy family. Walt Worthy and his wife have made an outstanding contribution to this exquisite and very elegant hotel. Love, labor, time and money have been poured into the once vacant hotel. Now Spokanites can proudly boast that the Davenport Hotel has been tastefully restored to its full glory and opulence.

JESSE AND VIRGINIA GROFF:

My mother's younger sister by almost four years is my Aunt Ginny. That was my nickname for Virginia. Aunt Ginny was born Virginia Schafer in 1921 at Deaconess Hospital. She resembled her mother, Ruby, even though she did not inherit, Ruby's luxurious auburn hair which came from Ruby's father, Chauncey Doyen. Aunt Ginny was known for being tall, skinny, and blessed with a thick head of honey blonde hair. In my eyes, she was prettier than all the famous Hollywood movie stars put together. Her make-up was always done to perfection. She wore the latest and the most fashionable clothes. Her hair was regularly permed and curled by well known hair stylists in Spokane. She could be seen wearing the latest and most popular coiffures. She was a knock-out to look at, no matter what the occasion. The nicest thing about my Aunt Ginny was her charming and pleasant personality. She had a rather calm, but sophisticated demeanor about her. Simply put, my aunt has always been a "knock out," and I have always adored her.

Aunt Ginny, like my mom, attended North Central High School, where she graduated in 1939. She was a cheerleader and considered to be one of the popular kids. She worked as an usherette at the Fox Theater in her spare time to earn spending money.

Shortly after the end of the war, Aunt Ginny was introduced to a handsome young banker, Jesse Groff, in Deer Park, by some close mutual friends, Ed and Lenore Meyers and Elizabeth Bacon. The handsome young man would later become my Uncle Jesse.

Uncle Jesse was raised in the small farming town of Springdale, Washington. When he returned from fighting in World War II, he discovered there was lots of competition for work in the small farming community. His former seventh and eight grade teacher recommended him to Charlie Snapp, the president of the local bank. Mr. Snapp liked Uncle Jesse. He hired him as a bank employee. Shortly after Jesse was hired to work at the bank in Springdale, Mr. Snapp decided to relocate the bank to Deer Park. Deer Park is a small little farming community about thirty miles north of Spokane. Uncle Jesse was grateful to have a job and learn the banking and financing business, even though it meant moving away from his home town.

As a kid growing up in a poor small farming community, it was difficult to earn much money. When Jesse graduated from the Springdale High School in 1937 he was making ten dollars a month. With this money he had to pay for his own clothes and food. Because of the limited financial opportunities in Springdale, Jesse joined the Army in December 1938 at Ft. George Wright in Spokane.

After two years at Ft. Wright, he was transferred to the 3rd Infantry Division at Fort Lewis near Tacoma, Washington. His battalion commanding officer in 1941 was Lieutenant Colonel Dwight D. Eisenhower. Just before the Japanese attacked Pearl Harbor, his battalion was sent to Southern California to guard the North American Aircraft plant and airfield located at Inglewood. His three year enlistment with the Army was up, nearing the time when the Japanese attacked Pearl Harbor on December 7, 1941. Consequently, his enlistment was immediately extended for the duration of World War II. His battalion commander, Lt. Colonel Eisenhower, was

Jesse and Virginia Groff with Karen, Steve, and Kevin. Picture taken in front of Ben and Ruby Schafer's fireplace in 1954.

then ordered to report to Washington, D.C. at the summons of General George C. Marshal.

When Jesse returned to Ft. Lewis with his unit, he was recommended by his company commander to attend officer candidate school. Jesse was accepted into the school and sent to Ft. Benning, Georgia in 1942. Upon graduation from O.C.S., he was commissioned a 2nd Lieutenant and assigned to the 9th Infantry Division at Fayetteville, North Carolina.

Before being shipped to North Africa to take part in the invasions of French Morocco, men of the 9th Infantry Division were given a pep talk by General George S. Patton, Jr. Shortly after the pep talk, First Lieutenant Jesse Groff landed on the North African coast in French Morocco in November 1942. This invasion was the first military action the U.S. Army took against the German Army in World War II. Lieutenant Groff and the 9th Infantry Division met the British 8th Army in Bizerta which spelled the end of the North African campaign. During this campaign, General George Patton, Jr. was assigned to be commander of the U.S. Army in North Africa.

In July 1943, Uncle Jesse landed in Sicily with the 9th Infantry Division. After the successful conclusion of the Sicilian campaign, Uncle Jesse and the 9th Infantry Division were sent to England to prepare for the invasion of France. During this period of time, his old battalion commander in 1941, Dwight Eisenhower, became the Supreme Allied Commander in Europe.

Three days after D-Day, June 6, 1944, Lt. Groff landed with units of the 9th Infantry Division in Normandy France to resume their fight against the German Army.

On June 22, 1944, Lieutenant Groff, in his capacity as executive officer to his company commander, was critically wounded by shrapnel during a German artillery barrage. His company was fighting near St. Mere Egliese, Normandy.

Jesse was dazed and in serious pain, but somehow managed to find enough strength to call for a medic. By some miracle, the medics were swift to respond to the struggling plea for help. Within a few minutes the medics were at his side. After assessing the seriousness of his wounds, the medics gave him morphine and carried him on a stretcher to the battalion headquarters.

Kevin Groff and Janice Magney taken at the home of Jesse and Virginia Groff. This picture was made into an oil portrait by Erna Bert.

Large hospital tents had been set up to care for the wounded.

According to Uncle Jesse, army jeeps were rigged up to act as substitute ambulances. Two stretchers were placed on top of the jeep. The seriously injured would be transported to a hospital tent that was used as a surgical station. As the soldiers were taken off of the ambulance, their stretchers would be placed on the dirt floor of the tent. As Lt. Groff was lying on the floor, a nurse and a young doctor came by to examine him. Not only did they detect the seriousness of his condition, but they realized he was an officer. Orders were given to get him ready for surgery immediately.

Reflecting back on that particular event, he remembers the staff giving him sodium penathol right before the surgery. He felt he received superior care by army nurses, even though the conditions were less than desirable. One of the first meals was served to him following surgery was a bowl of hot navy beans. He said that was one of the best meals he had eaten in a long time. Eventually, he was sent to another field hospital in Cherbourg, France, where he spent a week recuperating from the surgery. As his health improved and his condition was stabilized, he was flown to a US hospital in England, where he spent many months recovering from the extensive surgery on his legs and abdomen. Before his wounds had fully recovered, he received orders to report back to active duty.

About the time of the Battle of the Bulge, Lt. Groff was sent back to the hospital to remove more shrapnel from his body. At that time he became seriously ill with hepatitis, malaria and acquired keratitis in his right eye which became ulcerated. Eventually, he was transported to hospitals in North Carolina. By that time, he had fought in six different campaigns, and the military doctors believed that he was not fit of further combat. At Fort Bragg, he was given the choice of administrative (desk) duty or retirement. He was promoted to Captain and allowed to retire in 1946. Shortly after he was discharged, he returned to his home town of Springdale, Washington, and was soon introduced my Aunt Ginny.

The courtship of Aunt Ginny and Uncle Jesse lasted a little less than a year. They were married on May 29, 1947, at Grandma and Grandpa Schafer's home on Seventeenth Avenue.

For seven years, they made their home in Deer Park, and began their family. In 1954, Jesse went to work for Washington Trust Bank. During his banking career he managed two different branch banks and became the Assistant Vice President for Commercial Loans. They purchased a home on Twenty Sixth Avenue.

An event that will always live with members of our family is a picture that Uncle Jesse took of Kevin and Janice when they were two years old. The two tykes were sitting on the back porch of the Groff home eating watermelon. They were so engrossed with the delicious fruit that they were oblivious to anyone around them. Uncle Jesse grabbed the camera and snapped away. The black and white picture he took looked like a Norman Rockwell painting.

One day many years later, as Mom was showing the black and white snap shot to Eric and Erna Bert, Erna Bert was so impressed with the picture of Janice and Kevin, she insisted that she take the black and white photograph. Erna Bert enlarged the photograph and painted an 11x14 oil portrait for mom and dad and one for Aunt Ginny and Uncle Jesse. Today those portraits are family classics and bring back wonderful memories of days gone by. One of the portraits hangs on the living room wall of Jesse and Virginia. The other is now with Janice.

A Side Note.

As the years passed by, and their children grew, the house on 26th became too small for the family of five. Jesse built several homes for his family. A couple of those homes were on the far north side of Spokane, near Whitworth College. Virginia worked for Fidelity Savings and Loan, and eventually bought Helen's Styling Salon in Spokane Valley.

Today they are retired, and enjoy the company of their children, numerous grandchildren and great - grand children.

Their youngest son, Kevin, went to work for Safeway when he was fifteen years old, and currently is the Human Resource Director for Safeway Grocery Stores. Son Steve lives in Kent and works for the Attorney General's Office in downtown Seattle. Their daughter, Karen, and her husband, Mike, live in Spokane and are the owners of Mike's Saddle Shop.

SUNDAY DINNER AT
THE SPOKANE HOTEL

As a child growing up, the most important day of the week at the Magney home was Sunday. There was Sunday school that began at 9am followed by the 11am church service, followed by the family dinner at either the Davenport Hotel or the Spokane Hotel.

At 8:45, Dad had us kids piled into the old Ford Sedan, and in later years the big black Buick. Off we would head down Bernard Street, left on to Fourteenth and then right on to Cedar Street until, we reached the bottom of the hill at Fourth Avenue. Dad pulled up to First Presbyterian Church, parked the car and would take Richard, Janice and me into our appropriate Sunday school classrooms.

He would head back home, pick-up Mom, make the same return trip down the hill, and return in time for choir practice and pre choir socializing.

Mom would meet us after Sunday school, and take us for fresh doughnuts and fresh baked cookies in the coffee room. Grandpa Schafer was one of the ushers, so he would usually hold two pews for the family to sit together.

There was one particular Sunday that brings back special memories for me. Janice was about four years old. She was a tomboy, even though I always curled her hair on Saturday night, selected a frilly dress for church, and watched over her like a hawk. On this particular Sunday, she was extremely antsy and restless. No one was able to meet her every whim. She was seven years my junior and usually got her way with almost anything she wanted.

Mom and Aunt Mary were busy as church greeters. Dad was singing in the choir. Grandpa Schafer was ushering. Grandma and Grandpa Magney were seated next to Grandma Schafer. Uncle Jim (Winton) was busy rounding-up Jane and Judy. He apparently sensed that I was having problems with Janice. I was stressed to the max.

Janice was behaving very inappropriately in church. She was calling out for Mom and Dad, wiggling in the church pew, and intentionally bumping into the person sitting next to her. I am sure that if Mom had been present, this would not have happened. Just before the church service began, Uncle Jim had Grandpa Schafer arrange the seating so Janice was placed next to him in the church pew. Talk about a miracle from heaven. Uncle Jim had a wonderful sense of humor, and loved to be around kids. He liked to draw. His favorite thing to draw was clowns or cartoon characters. Uncle Jim pulled out a pencil and paper and entertained Janice through the entire service, drawing cartoon characters.

Following this particular service, Grandpa Magney wanted to take the entire family out for Sunday dinner at the Spokane Hotel. This was one of his favorite places to eat. The other was at the Davenport Hotel. Grandpa personally knew the chef, and Clarence Taylor, the dining room steward at the Spokane Hotel. Dad decided he had better call ahead and make reservations, because there were about twenty of us. We would need two round tables to accommodate this gang.

The Spokane Hotel, built in 1889, was an old landmark located at First and Stevens. The hotel was a seven story brick building that had aged gracefully through the years. According to The Spokesman-Review, "The hotel played host to the obscure, to the newcomers in town and to the world-renowned. People like William Jennings Bryan, Theodore Roosevelt, Herbert Hoover and practically every governor of Washington found their way to this remarkable old establishment. During its heyday it was lavish and elegant. Its meeting and banquet rooms at one time in the city's history were aglow with many of the city's most dazzling receptions and parties. The Spokane Hotel was a mecca and meeting place for many of Spokane's civic groups and service clubs."

As the years passed, it no longer was the showplace it once was. I remember the hotel had a simple lobby that was modestly elegant but comfortable. The ceiling of the main lobby was finished in redwood, and large columns were finished in marble. The guest registration office was in the northwest corner of the lobby.

What I remember most about the Spokane Hotel was the restaurant known as The Silver Grill. The restaurant had handsome murals, wrought iron light fixtures, dark beams and woodwork, with red tiled walls containing ornamental inlays. The décor was old English. One of its main features was a huge fireplace. The Silver Grill was elegant, with a masculine flair. The food was marvelous and the employees friendly. It was a charming place to go for an anniversary dinner, or have a special birthday celebration.

The staff at the Hotel was always wonderful to Grandma and Grandpa. They went out of their way to combine tables for this large family gathering. There were fine white linen table clothes with matching linen napkins, and fresh flowers on the tables. The staff had uniforms that were starched to the tee. The matre'd made a fuss over the family and personally pulled out the chairs for the two grandmothers first. I always wondered how he could be so quick as to know which chair to pull out next. Half way through our meal, the dining room steward, a big black man named Clarence Taylor, who was the "traveling carver," would come out to shake Grandpa Magney's hand and visit with the other adults in our party. I have wonderful memories of this jolly black man who was a gentle giant. He wore a big wide grin on his face along with his starched immaculate white uniform and his chef's cap. Clarence claimed the hearts of hundreds of the hotel's patrons. He started his career at the hotel when he was twelve years old by turning huge roasts of beef on a spit. He worked at The Silver Grill for more than fifty years. When Clarence became old enough, he was made a wine boy, and then a waiter. It was impressive to see Clarence and his huge silver traveling carver, move throughout the dining room with huge slabs of beef or immense glistening brown turkeys. According to mom, this large ornate silver traveling carver was almost one of a kind. It was purchased in France in 1902, just to be used at the Spokane Hotel. Clarence and the ornate silver traveling carver added a sense of class, dignity, and opulence, to the Silver Grill dining experience. Clarence also had a personality that made everyone feel important, even us kids.

As much as I enjoyed the atmosphere of the Silver Grill, many times these dinner parties seemed to be tiring and boring, especially when we had to sit like proper adults for long periods before the food was served. Because the staff seemed to sense our restlessness, they would offer us water or make small conversations with us.

On this particular Sunday, everything was pretty much the same as every Sunday, except Janice was becoming more restless and naughtier than ever. Halfway through the meal, she slid out of her chair and started to run around the table. She was quickly followed by her four year old cousin Kevin Groff. Before either set of parents could grab these two four year old rascals, they had bumped into a bus boy who was carrying a stack of dishes back to the kitchen, and knocked into a waitress who was carrying food to other tables. Well, disaster struck hard. There was the clanging and rattling of dishes while food went flying through the air. As Daddy was quickly grasping Janice's arm, she raised her free arm, knocked a glass of water out of Grandma Magney's hand. Water went flying everywhere! It soaked the front of her dress, the table cloth and my mother, who was sitting beside her. Horror struck Grandma's face, and Mom's big green eyes almost popped out of her head with anger! "Janice Ellen," my mother shrieked at the top of her lungs, "look what you have done!"

Poor Grandpa Magney was so embarrassed and humiliated! I remember him apologizing to the waitress and the matre'd for the behavior of his grandkids. That Sunday he left a hefty tip on the table. Dad and Uncle Jess dug deep into their pockets to add to the tip as they were exiting the dining room. Financially speaking, it ended up being a profitable day for the dining room staff. The Magney family certainly provided entertainment for the other Sunday diners; however, it probably was not the type of entertainment they were seeking. As for Janice Ellen, well, let's just say it ended up being a very bad day for her rear end.

A Side Note.

By the mid fifties, many changes were taking place in Spokane due to a word called 'progress.' The Spokane Hotel eventually felt the sting of the wrecking ball as it plunged into the brick building in 1970. Today, in its place stands the Ridpath Hotel, which has remained a well- established hotel in downtown Spokane.

THE WINTON FAMILY:
The rags to riches story

The year was 1946 when we first met. I can't recall what that first meeting was like, but I am sure Aunt Mary and Uncle Jim remember it well. My guess is that it was shortly after I was born.

This story, however, begins many years before I was even the "twinkle in my father's eye."

God has mysterious ways of working many unusual miracles of love and grace by creating families of unique individuals who are not related to one another biologically. I have come to believe that bringing people together who have been total strangers is one of God's specialties. The story of the Magneys and the Wintons is such a story. It is a story of God's great love for church and its believers. It's a story about a binding love that can't be explained, only experienced.

The relationship between Jack and Dorothy Magney and Jim and Mary Winton began at First Presbyterian Church in the late thirties.

The story begins with the birth of Jim Winton in Portland, Oregon on January 18, 1905. His father Eugene had a drinking problem, and when Jim was no more than three years old, his mother Rebecca told his father to leave. His father begged for forgiveness, but Rebecca stood firm with her decision. There would be no reconciliation in their marriage.

A couple of years later, his mother married a man who would eventually become abusive to Rebecca and her two children.

The home in which Jim was raised was very small and simple. The first floor of the home was an all dirt floor. His bedroom was up in the attic. It was in that room of the house that he learned to operate a ham radio set and spent many hours sketching cartoon faces on pieces of paper.

When Jim was seven and eight years old he experienced severe stomach problems due to emotional upsets and an unhappy childhood. This illness kept him out of school for almost a year.

As a youngster, he attended Fourth Presbyterian Church in Portland. It was here that he acquired a love for the Lord, and developed a life time devotion to the church.

At 13 years old, he took on a busy paper route in order to help support the family. One day when delivering the paper to the Court House in Portland, he fell down the Court House steps and broke his leg. Once again it would mean that Jim would not be able to attend school. This time, he missed almost four months of school.

When he graduated from Benson Poly Tech School in 1923, he left home. He could no longer stand the intolerable living conditions of his youth. He enrolled at Oregon State College. It was there that he supported himself by drawing cartoons for the school magazine, The Owl. He also repaired pipe organs for churches. The money he earned went for college tuition and housing. He proudly boasts that during those struggling college years he lived on Cheerio cereal for breakfast, lunch and dinner.

In 1928, he finally graduated from Oregon State University with a degree in Electrical Engineering. Immediately following his graduation, Uncle Jim went to work for Pacific Power & Light in Pasco, Washington and Lewiston, Idaho. Then, in 1931, he moved to Spokane and went to work for Washington Water Power.

Due to his charming, outgoing personality, a marvelous sense of humor and his ability to teach, Washington Water Power felt it would be beneficial to have Uncle Jim work in the sales department, educating the public on the advantages of having an all-electric home.

During the early thirties, the majority of homes in Spokane were heated with coal furnaces. The housewife washed the clothes using old fashion ringer washing machines. To dry the clothes, women would hang the clothes outside on a clothes line. Many kitchens still contained the wood burning stove, and food was refrigerated in an ice box. With electrical power becoming more affordable to home owners throughout the state of Washington, the Spokane housewife saw the advantage of owning electrical appliances and was most eager to convert to an electrical home. In the name of progress and new technology, Jim Winton helped educate many Spokane families on the benefits of owning electrical appliances. Women were anxious to get rid of the old -fashioned, out- dated iceboxs and purchase new modern electrical refrigerators. Refrigerators did not need the large blocks of ice to keep the food cold. Electrically, the refrigerator would keep the temperatures at a colder and safer level. This meant that it was easier to store foods more safely and for longer periods of time. This also meant that the average woman did not have to make a daily trip to the grocery store and purchase perishable foods.

While busy working for WWP during the day, Jim Winton kept himself busy at night by attending Gonzaga Law School. In 1935, he graduated from Gonzaga University with a degree in Law.

Many romances begin in the work place. This was true for Uncle Jim. The women at WWP were always flirting with the tall, handsome, curly haired bachelor.

Aunt Mary also worked for Washington Water Power in the Purchasing Department from 1937 to 1945. Aunt Mary was born to George and Opha Graham on March 26, 1910 in Spokane, Washington. Like Mom, she graduated from North Central High School. She then went on to Kinman Business College for two years of business education.

Following high school, women in the thirties, forties and fifties usually had one of three choices to further their education. You could go to college to become a teacher, attend nursing school, or enroll in a reputable business college. Mary Elizabeth Graham chose the last option.

After a few years of working in the sales department for Washington Water Power, Uncle Jim's duties and responsibilities expanded. He was promoted to an engineer, supplying electricity to homes and businesses in eastern Washington and northern Idaho.

Safety and first aid was a priority for this rapidly expanding electrical company. Washington Water Power added a safety department, and recruited staff from other departments to assist with the teaching and training of first aid to other employees. Jim was assigned the task being the captain of the men's first aid team. He enjoyed overseeing the men's first aid team so much that he volunteered to be the coach for the ladies first aid team.

It was when Uncle Jim was coaching the ladies first aid team that he first noticed Mary, who had volunteered to be one of the victims to be treated by the first aid team. I guess one could say there was a spark of electricity between the petite little Mary and the six-foot-three engineer. Their romance was aided by the singles group at First Presbyterian Church that Jack and Dorothy Magney belonged to, before their marriage in 1940.

I am not sure when or how Uncle Jim proposed to Aunt Mary, but I do know that before Jim Winton and Mary Graham were married, they joined First Presbyterian Church. Both immediately became very active and involved in the life and growth of the church. Jim and Mary exchanged wedding vows at First Presbyterian Church on August 12, 1941.

Aunt Mary and Uncle Jim were not your typical young couple when they became husband and wife. They were somewhat older than many of their married friends when they exchanged wedding nuptials. Both had worked for a number of years and set aside money for the future. While Mary was working, she was also taking care of her ailing mother, Opha. Shortly after Opha passed away, Jim and Mary tied the knot. As newly weds, they desired to begin a family immediately.

Conception was easy for Aunt Mary, but keeping the pregnancy was another matter. After experiencing numerous miscarriages during the first six years of their marriage, Mary and Jim made a crucial decision in their lives to start looking into the possibility of adopting a baby.

Sadly, they were turned down by all of the adoption agencies in Spokane, because they were considered to be "too old" to be raising a family. Adoption agencies in the forties believed that younger couples made better parents. Uncle Jim was in his early forties and Aunt Mary was in her mid thirties when they began their discouraging search for a baby.

One day, Mary and Jim received a phone call from Uncle Jim's sister, Bernice Sitton, who worked in a medical lab at a hospital in Portland. She had recently learned from one of the physicians about a baby who was going to be put-up for adoption. The young mother to be was willing to let the attending physician locate a Christian couple to adopt her baby. If Mary and Jim were interested, Bernice would talk with the attending physician and assist in any way possible with the adoption arrangements. Immediately, they made a quick trip to Portland, Oregon to meet with the young woman's doctor, and began the process of filling-out the adoption papers. Now all they had to do was sit back and wait for that thrilling phone call.

For Aunt Mary, who so badly wanted a baby, the few short weeks seemed to drag on and on. Finally, in January, 1947 they received the exciting phone call they had been anticipating. They could come and get their new baby girl. Jim and Mary quickly packed their belongings and rushed off to Portland to meet their new four day old daughter, Judy.

There is nothing like having a new baby in a home to either increase one's stress level or reduce it. In the case of Jim and Mary, baby Judy must have brought so much joy and happiness to their lives that Mary found herself once again pregnant. Nineteen months later on June 17th, at Saint Lukes Hospital, Jim and Mary hit the jackpot. Mary gave birth to a little daughter named Jane. At long last, the Winton's were a family of four.

In 1947, Uncle Jim was ordained an Elder at First Presbyterian Church. Through the years, he devoted many hours of service to this wonderful church as its attorney and consultant.

He was very instrumental in obtaining the property for the Sunday School building addition that was built in 1952.

As I understand it, the lady who owned a portion of the property refused to sell the property to the Church. Ironically, Uncle Jim knew the lady's son, Manny. Manny and Uncle Jim had attended Oregon State College, and were roommates. When the two graduated from Oregon State University in 1928, their lives went in different directions for a few years.

It wasn't until the early 1950's that Manny and Uncle Jim were reunited and rekindled their friendship. One day while joking and visiting when

Manny was in town, Uncle Jim told Manny about his latest project at the church and all the trouble he was having because the owner, an elderly lady, refused to sell. When Manny found out it was the property adjacent to the church and his mother's house, he told Jim that he could probably help him and the church solve his problem. Jim informed Manny the church was prepared to make a substantial financial offer to his mother regarding purchasing her home. Elder Winton explained that First Presbyterian Church needed her land so they could build an addition on to the church, and build a Sunday school classroom for all the children who were attending the church.

Like all churches in America, after World War II, First Presbyterian Church grew by leaps and bounds. With numerous new families and a zillion little tykes, the old church building was bursting at its seams. Uncle Jim's charm prevailed, and Manny's mother accepted the church offer. In 1952 the new addition and Sunday school building was completed.

Through the years, Uncle Jim had numerous interests including politics. In 1954, he was elected to the Washington State House of Representatives where he served for one term. Another passion was education. He served on the School Board for District 81 for many years, and served as its president for eight years. At home, his passions were his wife, two daughters and gardening. Like grandpa Schafer, Uncle Jim had a love for flowers, especially peonies.

Jim and Mary Winton with daughters Jane on the left and Judy on the right. Family picture was used by Jim when he was running as a Replican candidate for Congress in the fourth district.

121

Jim was a man of many talents. One of those talents was his ability to draw cartoon characters and entertain people with his wit and drawings. On many occasions, he would position himself in between us kids during the church service and keep us quiet by drawing cartoons or send notes to us. He always managed to have two or three children on each side of him.

He also enjoyed going for walks in the neighborhood. He purposely had Oreo cookies in his pant pockets to give to the kids he would run into. It was not long before had had quite a following.

Uncle Jim was a tease, and when I was six or seven years of age he nick-named me "MM." I was never sure if "MM" was for Marilyn Magney or Marilyn Monroe. After that, I always referred to my Uncle Jim as "JW."

Mom and Aunt Mary were inseparable. They could almost have been re-ferred to as the "Bobbsey Twins." They belonged to the same women's church circle known as Lucia Pratt. They worked on the Presbyterian Women's As-sociation. They taught Sunday school classes together, and always signed-up to be church greeters together. When Judy and I approached junior high age, it was Mom and Aunt Mary who recruited Dad and JW to help them with the volunteer job of leaders and counselors for the junior high youth group meetings at First Pres.

As close as Mom and Aunt Mary were to one another, they were as oppo-site as day and night. Mom loved her home and thrived on entertaining, cre-ating gourmet delicacies and growing beautiful flowers. Aunt Mary was not the least bit interested in any of these tasks. She should have been given the title of transportation coordinator for the church, the Red Cross, friends and family. Mom, the church or us kids were always asking Aunt Mary to take us to one place or another.

As unbelievable as this will sound, Dorothy Magney never learned how to drive a car. I guess she never needed to because Aunt Mary seemed to be our full time chauffer. Whenever someone from church was ill and needed a meal delivered to their home, it was Aunt Mary that the church called. This, of course, meant that Mom prepared the food, and Mary Winton acted as the delivery person.

Aunt Mary was diminutive in size, and often reminded me of a little fox terrier. She was very hyper and could not sit still. Staying at home was not her cup of tea. She was constantly on the move, thrived on taking on a new challenge, and never knew how to say "NO." I am not sure she knew what the word meant, because it never seemed to be part of her vocabulary.

Jim and Mary Winton raised Jane and Judy in an unpretentious one-story home that sat on the corner of Forty First and South Sherman. Their lives were a reflection of simplicity coupled with hard work, and devotion to family, church and community.

When growing up, there was never a day that went by that Mom did not talk to Aunt Mary. If they were not on the phone with one another, then Aunt Mary was at our house with Judy and Jane. Dad had great admiration for JW, and frequently turned to him for legal and spiritual advice. Both men shared a commitment to Christ and the church.

SEVERAL SIDE NOTES.

Here is a drawing and a poem that JW sent to Aunt Mary shortly after they were married (*page 124*).

On numerous occasions church members would ask Mom or Aunt Mary how they were related. They always gave the same answer, smiled, and walked away leaving most people in a perplexed state of wonderment. There famous response was, "We are related through our children!!!"

The real truth is that God brought these Christian couples together and anointed them with an everlasting love for one another.

Eventually, Jim became a legal research analyst for Washington Water Power Company. During his career, he experienced several disappointments, yet never became discouraged. During one point in his legal career, he was passed up for a judgeship in Spokane County. While working for Washington Water Power Company, one of his goals had been to become President of the company. This did not happen. After working for 42 years for Washington Water Power, he decided it was time for him to retire or 'sort of retire.' When I say 'sort of,' I am referring to the fact that he no longer was working for the Water Power Company, but instead joined the legal team at Col. Clarence Orndorff's office, where he worked for an additional ten years.

The story of Jim Winton is truly a rags to riches story. He was a self made man who worked hard and studied hard. In all that he did, he gave God the credit for his successes and blessings. The old hymn, I WILL SING THE WONDEROUS STORIES OF THE CHRIST WHO DIED FOR ME, is a reflection of how Jim Winton lived his life for the Lord.

```
There once was a young romeo named Jim
Who maintained his bachelorhood with vigor and vim
          Then he met the girl
          With the brownish curl
And now she's made a married man out of him.


There was a sweet young lady named Mary
Who wasted no time on every Tom, Dick and Harry
          She found her Jim
          And hung on to him
And now Mary he recently did marry.


Although his department with beauteous gals was staft
At the thought of losing his heart, Jim W. laught
          Then came along Mary G.
          He lost it completely
And now there's less danger he'll get caught in the draft.
```

Jim Winton's character sketch and poem to Mary Graham Winton before they were married.

THE WORLD OF RETIREMENT

There was a facet of life in the '40s and '50s that I feel compelled to mention. It was an important part of society although it did not dramatically affect me as a child. Yet it played a minor roll in my life in the '50s, and would go on to play an even larger role in my adult life. I am referring to the world of retirement homes.

My first actual recollection of hearing about retirement living was when I listened to an in-depth conversation between Grandma and Grandpa Schafer, when they considered going into such a home.

Both grandparents were active Presbyterians and somewhat involved with the Inland Empire Presbytery. A good friend, L.J. Harger, was the Treasurer for Presbyterian Synod of Alaska Northwest. Mr. Harger apparently had been sharing information with the grandparents about the possibility of the Synod purchasing property owned by Whitworth College, for the sole intent of building a retirement community for those over the age of 62. The land was on Hawthorne Road, east of Division Street.

At the June 17, 1957 meeting of Presbyterian Ministries Inc. Board of Trustees, it was voted to approve the purchase of 5.6 acres of land from Whitworth College for the price of $3,000 per acre. On a later date, some of the Trustees such as Albert Arend, an elder at Knox Presbyterian Church, Synod Executive, Rev. Clarence Polhemus, and Elden Unruh voted to approve ground breaking as soon as January 1, 1958. They were in hopes the one-story building, with studio, and one bedroom apartments, would be ready for occupancy no later than October 1958. The one-story building would have a large restaurant like dining room that would be opened for breakfast, lunch and dinner. At the front entry to the building would be a cozy lounge with floor to ceiling windows and a large fireplace, where guests and residents could talk and socialize. In a separate wing of the building would be an infirmary, staffed with nurses 24 hours a day in case a resident became ill.

Grandma was very excited about this new concept. Several of her close lady friends had already signed up to move into the new building in 1958. She loved the thought that all three meals would be provided. Housekeepers would come and clean their apartment, and best of all, she would be near some of her friends.

My heart sank when I thought about Grandma and Grandpa leaving their beautiful big home on 17th near the park.

Grandpa was one-hundred-percent opposed to the idea. He did not want to give up his newly built green house, or his job, for retirement living.

I also recall that my parents discouraged such a move, but I had no way of knowing why.

At the same time the Presbyterians were building their retirement community on the north side of town, the Methodists were also in the process of developing and building a retirement community on the South Hill less than a mile from my home on 22nd Street. Many times I pedaled my bike up the hill to 25th to observe this tower being built.

Grandma did not give up on her idea of retirement living. If Grandpa would not consider moving out to the far north side of town, maybe he would consider moving to another location on the south side. During the past year she had been acquiring detailed information about the new home the Methodists were building.

On December 14, 1956, Mr. Arthur W. Sherwood, Special Assistant for Housing for the Elderly in Washington, D.C. of the Federal housing Administration, was in Spokane to conduct a meeting arranged by the Spokane office of the FHA.

Dr. Richard D. Decker, then Superintendent of the Spokane District of the Methodist Church, and Mr. O.W. Young, a local layman of the

Methodist Church, were there to listen to Mr. Sherwood's presentation.

Mr. Sherwood told his audience of a law passed by Congress which provides for Federal Housing Administration support to finance housing for senior citizens.

The two gentlemen became interested in this new concept and presented the idea to Methodist Annual Conference.

Mr. Young came to Spokane in 1906 from Minnesota where he had worked for the YMCA. During his career he had worked as the Deputy Auditor, Clerk of the Board of County Commissioners, and as a Commissioner. Later he was appointed a Land Appraiser for the state of Washington.

A committee of fourteen was formed to study the possibility of building such a home in Spokane. A meeting was held at Central Methodist Church to discuss the concept and the location. After a location had been selected, it was decided to sign incorporation papers and give the corporation the name of "Spokane Methodist Homes Inc."

At a later date, thirty-two acres of land were purchased. Then, an additional 40 acres of land directly west of the original 32 acres was secured.

At a meeting in August, 1957 the name Rockwood Manor was suggested by Mr. John Young. Eventually, architects and contractors were selected, and building began on this ten-story retirement building. The new Methodist retirement home was scheduled to open in late 1959 or early 1960.

Grandma was not able to convince Grandpa that living in a retirement community on the south side or north side was a good idea. He was not going to give up his roses, begonias, and orchids. Nor did he have plans to quit his job with URM, even though he was a young seventy.

I was most curious about these new heated family discussions, or debates. I wanted to know what was so special or unusual about this new concept called retirement living.

According to grandma, in days prior to the 20s and 30s, there usually was no place for an elderly person to go if he or she needed assistance, except into the home of children or siblings, or into what was referred to as the Poor Farm. Listening to grandma's horror stories, this state supported institution was obviously not something to be wished for by anyone.

Hawthorne Retirement Community built by Presbyterian Ministries Inc., in the fifties. Today the CCRC is owned by Spokane United Methodist Homes and is known as Rockwood at Hawthorne.

This drawing is of Rockwood Retirement Community which was built in the late fifties. Today it is known as Rockwood South and is owned by Spokane United Methodist Homes.

In the 1940s churches and some fraternities began to understand the need to provide dignified care for elderly men and women and retirement homes began to be built. They ranged in size and service from the simplest room-only home to the more elaborate Continuing Care Retirement Community (CCRC) which provided extensive care and services.

Originally, as the concept of independence for older people began to take hold, it was deemed more desirable to have a facility completely separate from any thought of illness or health care. Perish the thought that these happy, healthy men and women would ever need more care.

But reality set in quickly. Homes began to provide independence, but also the health care needed as people aged in place.

Hawthorn Manor, a Presbyterian home; Rockwood Manor, a Methodist home; and Riverview Terrace, a Lutheran home were the first three CCRCs to be built in Spokane and were among the first in the nation to become leaders in this new independence-for-seniors thinking. Among the many leaders in this field was Robert Zachow, a Presbyterian layman and accountant, who became Administrator of the new Lutheran Riverview Terrace Retirement Home. He was among the first to begin teaching others that administration of such homes was a highly specialized matter that required specific skills and training, as opposed to what some church leaders had believed—that all that was required was a devoted and dedicated retired pastor.

SEVERAL SIDE NOTES.

Little did I realize that many years later I would chose to work in the very specialized profession of providing care and service to the elderly. Ironic as it may seem, I became Administrator of Hawthorne Manor. I was hired by Mr. Zachow's wife, Betty. For a number of years, we both worked for Presbyterian Ministries and Arthur G. Langley, CEO, son of a former Governor of Washington State.

Today, Hawthorne Manor is known as Rockwood at Hawthorne. In 1997, Presbyterian Ministries sold the community to Spokane United Methodist Homes which owns Rockwood Retirement Community.

Neither sets of grandparents, the Magneys or the Schafers, seemed to understand the word *Retirement.* Grandpa Magney worked until he was 90 years old managing the Brunot Hall apartments. Grandpa Schafer retired from URM at 82.

According to Grandpa Schafer, he couldn't find the word 'retirement' in the Bible. Abraham was ninety nine when God told him he would be the "Father of many nations." He was one hundred years old, and Sarah was ninety, when Isaac was born. Noah, by our standards today, was ancient when he obeyed God's calling to build the Ark. Moses was an old man when he wrote the 10 Commandments and led his people out of Egypt.

SPOKANE'S WONDERFUL PARKS

During my childhood, my greatest love was to play at the many wonderful parks that surrounded our home on 22nd Street. I didn't need to have a street or backyard to play in. God blessed the Magney family by giving them the good fortune to have the biggest backyards at their finger tips; Manito and Comstock Parks. The Coeur d'Alene Park was another playground I enjoyed when visiting Grandma and Grandpa Magneys at the Brunot Hall apartments. This park was less than a half block away. It was directly across the street from the Patsy Clark Mansion.

There are more than 75 parks and pathways in Spokane that were landscaped with natural beauty, flower gardens picnic areas, ice skating ponds, swimming pools, and all sorts of recreational beauty.

It all began in 1891, when J.J. Browne and A. M. Cannon gave Spokane a piece of land west of Spokane Falls for its first public park, which was named Coeur d' Alene Park. The Coeur d' Alene Park, a rectangular piece of property, is located in Browne's Addition along Second Avenue between Chestnut and Spruce. It is Spokane's oldest park and the foundation for Spokane's current Park System. In the early days, croquet and horseshoes were among the games played on the park's grounds. At the turn of the century, the park contained lawn plantings, ornamental shrubbery, a fish pond, a wading pool, a rustic gazebo and a fancy onion-domed band pavilion. It was a true testament to Victorian splendor, and was the center for neighborhood relaxation.

In 1891, the parks came under the supervision of the Mayor and City Council. Sixteen years later, in 1907, the Board of Park Commissioners was established to oversee public park affairs. John C. Olmstead Jr., and his brother, both landscape architects from Brookline, Massachusetts, were commissioned to provide Spokane with a master plan for Spokane's Park Commissioners.

In the book, *Manito Park A Reflection of Spokane's Past,* Tony Bamonte and Suzanne Schaefer Bamonte state that "Mr. Aubrey White was the first President of the Spokane Park Board and eventually became known as the "Father of Spokane's Park System." He campaigned for twenty six years to beautify the city and develop its parks. Mr. White was responsible for obtaining undeveloped land at Riverside State Park, and Mount Spokane State Park. He was also responsible for hiring John Duncan to be the superintendent of the Spokane Park System. Mr. Duncan served as the superintendent for thirty two years. At Manito Park, near 21st and Park Drive where a dirt pit once existed, he began transforming the sunken area into a gorgeous array of perfectly carved and manicured flower beds. In 1941, the year before John Duncan retired the park board honored him by naming the gardens, Duncan Gardens."

It was always fun to walk along Park Drive and count the number of cars parked along the drive. I took great pleasure in reading the car license plates. To my amazement, many of those cars were from States beyond Washington.

My entertainment was not in observing the magnificent flowers and flower beds, but instead, my thrill was to remove my socks and shoes, and go wading in the famous Davenport Fountain that was located in the very middle of the beautiful flower beds. More than once, I was yelled at by the gardeners who were rearranging flowers and pruning shrubs. I was told to "get out of the fountain as it was not a public wading pool for kids to play in!" A day or so later, I would be back at the park, and once again try my luck at sticking my feet into this fountain while anticipating the splashing of water from the waterfall in the fountain, and hoping not to be caught.

On 29th near Bernard, but closer to Monroe Street, is a large park known as Comstock Park. This park had an Olympic size swimming pool and the largest slide and swings-sets in the entire city (and possibly in all of eastern Washington) in the early 50s. People from all parts of Spokane would come to swim at least once each summer at Comstock. The park was situated on 35 acres of land. Scattered throughout the park are baseball diamonds, tennis courts, numerous picnic tables and park benches. It had some of the largest Ponderosa Pine trees in the city. It was a fun park where families could bring their children to swim and play and enjoy a picnic lunch, although it lacked gardens, rolling hills and majestic water fountains. It was at this pool that I developed very good swimming skills.

Manito Park was only a hop, skip, and jump from 22nd Street. Part of the park started at Grand Boulevard near 16th, and continued south as far as 25th. The park was situated on 90 acres of land on Grand Boulevard, and then went west as far as Bernard Street, between 18th and 21st. At 21st, ,the park then jogged east to Park Drive and then up to 25th. Within the park are many roads and loop drives that travel throughout the entire park.

Manito Park is a main tourist attraction for Spokane. People from all over the United States come to visit the magnificent array of flower gardens in the summer months. The Park is divided into various sections that have well maintained roads and walking paths for the public. There can be found the Joel E. Ferris Perennial Gardens, Rose Hill, the Green House (now known as the Gaiser Conservatory), the Lilac Gardens, the Upper Manito Playground, and the famous Duncan Gardens. Interspersed between the gardens are rolling steep hills that provided the perfect environment for sledding or tobogganing every winter. At the North end of the Park is the Duck Pond which during Spokane's frigid winters, becomes a gigantic skating pond.

The Duck Pond, which was only four blocks from our home, was my favorite places to visit in both the summer and winter. According to The Spokesman-Review story regarding Manito Park's 100th Anniversary, the original Duck Pond at Manito Park was not a pond, but a spring fed lake. In the early history of the park, the lake was referred to as Mirror Lake and extended all the way to Grand Boulevard. The main body of water was the current Duck Pond but there was a canal that extended to the east near Grand. During the hot summer months, this canal would dry up leaving a stagnant infested Mosquito swamp. In 1912, in order to contain the water level, a concrete wall was built along the north and west sides of the lake. By doing this, the lake became a very large duck pond. Where Mirror Lake used to extend to Grand Boulevard, the Duck Pond was now located on 18th about four blocks west from Grand Boulevard.

The pond was surrounded by large grassy areas and a variety of old well established trees such as maple, weeping willow, and pine.

Large flat lily pads made it an ideal hiding and breeding place for frogs, turtles and gold fish. Because the pond provided this type of natural habitat, it attracted a large number of ducks each summer.

It was a common sight in the spring to see a mother duck swimming about the pond with her little ducklings in tow. A bag of bread crumbs and a few minutes to enjoy was all it took for a delightful trip to feed these little families. When Richard and I were between the ages of five, and eight, mom made it a regular weekly treat for us to feed the ducks. After Janice was born, we would load up her stroller with a picnic basket, and head for the duck pond to enjoy a lunch in the park.

In the winter months we loved to go ice skating at the Duck Pond. Located at the far west side of the pond was a huge basalt rock fireplace. This became the central spot to gather for a few minutes of warmth before going back out on to the ice. For those who loved to ice skate and experience the cold nip of the outdoors, the duck pond was the popular place to visit.

Reflecting back on those special days, I remember Dad loading up the car with me, Lija Zilgme, Arlene Allers, and her twin sisters Judy, and Jackie. We'd pile in the car with extra scarves, socks, mittens and of course our skates. We were ready for an exhilarating day of ice skating in the park.

The winters in Spokane were usually very cold. We could almost always count on a snow accumulation of a couple of feet from the end of October to mid March. Therefore, with each winte,r it was a regular past time to enjoy outdoor winter sports at the park.

Lija was by far the most athletic of all of us, and was a beautiful and graceful skater. The twins, too, were talented and graceful. And then there was me. Nimble, poised and elegant on a pair of ice skates I was not. I was great at stumbling over my own two feet and falling in front of other skaters. In fact, I probably fell more often on the ice than all the other skaters put together.

It became a practice for the other ice skaters to stay clear when I was on the ice, as I was always tripping over my own two feet and knocking other skaters down. My feet were always freezing, regardless of how many pairs of socks I had on my feet. I spent more time at the basalt fireplace warming my hands and my feet than actually skating. Ice skating was not my thing. But I loved the camaraderie of my friends, and was not about to be left behind. If the truth were to be told, I lived for the moment when Dad or Mr. Allers came to pick us girls up, and we piled back into the car and headed for home.

I think Dad and Howard Allers had as much fun as we did as they took us kids to and from the pond and other areas of the park, so we could enjoy the snow and winter outdoor sports.

Little did we appreciate how rare this adventure truly was, nor did we recognize the equally rare experience of ice skating on "our own" pond in our extended back yard for many years.

NATATORIUM PARK

Natatorium Park was Spokane's "Coney Island" and summer evening fun center. I can recall many happy hours spent there. As a child, the most magical thing in the whole world was to visit Natatorium Park every summer.

The park was located on the North side of the Spokane River in an area west of the Spokane Courthouse and down toward the Spokane River. The 50 some acres of park with rolling hills sat amid the river's towering pine trees.

As a park, Natatorium dates back to long before Spokane's destructive fire of August 4, 1889. In the early 1880's, the park site was known as Ingersall's Park, and eventually changed to Twickhenham Park. The Twickhenham name was to honor a popular amusement park near London, England.

According to numerous stories written by The Spokesman-Review, in 1887 a Spokane capitalist J.D. Sherwood, financed a cable car venture to the tune of $250,000 that carried passenger traffic from the original Northern Pacific Depot site to north Boone. There the cable lines turned west to travel the length of the Boone residential district to the crest above Natatorium.

In 1892, three years after the Spokane fire, the Spokane Street Railroad Co. bought the Boone Avenue cable line and its franchise. With the deal it acquired Twickhenham Park. The new park owners envisioned a miniature Coney Island-type amusement park.

The Spokesman Review also stated that park officials sought the help and assistance of Charles Looff, a Danish woodcarver who had designed some of the amusement concessions at Seattle's Luna Park at its Alki Point site on Pudget Sound. Today, Loof is one of the legends of American Carousel history. His figures and carvings are priceless and sought after in all parts of the country by antique collectors.

Looff made a sales pitch to the Water Power Co. that what Natatorium Park needed was a merry-go-round. The arrangement was agreed upon, and Looff spent two years building his merry-go-round. The name for the park was again changed by the park board. The new name was now Natatorium Park. Each year, new amusement attractions were added to enhance the profitability and attract larger crowds of people.

According to Grandma and Grandpa Schafer, Natatorium Park provided a magical playground for Spokane citizens and tourists for almost three quarters of a century. During the formative years, the park was a picnic ground, nature conservatory, had a performance pavilion and amusement rides. Mom and Dad told stories, about listening to John Philip Sousa concerts, swimming in the indoor heated pool, and in the evening attending a dance at the dance hall. They would flock to the dance pavilion with other young couples to hear Tommy Dorsey and other famous dance bands play the popular swing music. On the Fourth of July, many families visited the park to view the brilliant fire works display.

Twice during the summer, we visited Natatorium Park. On one occasion, Eric Van Werald would load up his station wagon with the gang of kids on 22nd Street and off to Nat Park we would go. We were the happiest bunch of kids in the entire city of Spokane. Mother and Aunt Mary also planned an annual summer outing for Jane, Judy, Richard, Janice and myself. Usually this occurred in the month of August, when they assumed the five of us might be getting somewhat bored with summer vacation, which of course held no truth at all.

During our annual summer outing, Mom and Aunt Mary made it a ritual to recount the history of Natatorium Park to us kids. As Aunt Mary was driving us to and from the Park, the five of us kids had to sit quietly in the back seat and listen to these two women recount the stories. There were stories of how Dad courted Mom at the park, and how Uncle Jim did the same when dating Aunt Mary. As children we were neither interested nor impressed with listening to the memories of their dating years. But as I have aged, and the grand amusement park was sold in the 70's to be replaced with a Senior Retirement Park, it is now fun to recount the historical stories.

For me there are many memories of nostalgic childhood rides on the old merry-go-round where Grandpa Schafer had courted Grandma, and where he also proposed to her. I thrilled to ride the jackrabbit, play on the bumper cars, fly in the Roll-a-Plane, twirl in the Octopus, ride into the spooky abyss of Fun in the Dark and then pretend I was taking my first continental train ride via the miniature railroad train.

As I mentioned earlier, Mom and Aunt Mary planned an annual all day outing for us kids at Natatorium Park. We all lived for the moment when that great day arrived. Aunt Mary would pull up to the house in her swept-wing 1956 Plymouth sedan. Jane and Judy would bounce out of the car, come running into the house and help us carry the baskets of food to put into the trunk. Mom prepared the food, which meant we had baskets and sacks all over the kitchen table. Aunt Mary furnished the pop, paper plates and silver ware. Within minutes, we were off for a full day of great fun and excitement. Nat Park here we come!

Every year, we tried to coax our mothers into buying more tickets than purchased the previous year. As we grew older, we believed we should be allowed to stay longer, which of course meant more of the amusement rides would be calling our name and waiting for our bodies to occupy a seat on the rides.

The usual routine for our Natatorium day would begin by locating the right parking place. We made great attempts to arrive early enough to get the best parking place closest to the picnic tables. Next was the challenge of finding the perfect picnic table for our gang. There was always a lot of dispute about this. Aunt Mary and Mom always preferred the tables that were in the shady areas of the park. Judy, Jane, Richard, and I liked the sunshine. It was our goal, however, to find picnic tables that weren't too far from the parking lot, but close to the amusement rides. Following the selection of the picnic table, we then received the thrill of purchasing our tickets.

We were so excited to get to the amusement park rides that we inhaled our food. Our mothers were in no rush, and took their dear sweet time to enjoy the meal and share with each other the latest church and family news. This, of course frustrated the life out of us kids. But finally the ultimate moment would arrive - the distribution of the tickets. Before passing out the tickets, the ground rules were laid down for us kids. Judy and I were the oldest and, therefore, responsible for the welfare of Jane and Richard, who were eighteen months younger. Janice always stayed with mom and Aunt Mary because she was seven years younger than me.

There is one summer that will always live in my mind because Judy and I decided not to follow the rules established by our mothers. After all, we were getting older, and it was embarrassing to be seen with younger siblings. We were becoming mature girls of ten and eleven years of age. Judy and I planned our strategy all summer long on how we would attack this situation and basically ignore the rules our mothers would make. We devised our own game plan. When the moment was right, we would strike. The tickets had just been handed out to Jane and Richard and next to Judy and me. Instead of waiting for the instructions from our mothers, Judy and I took our tickets and immediately ran down the hill and headed directly to the jack rabbit. We hoped we could have at least two full rides on the roller coaster before our mothers would get anywhere close to us. Our next goal was to reach the Octopus, then to the Bumper Cars, and then on to the Fun in the Dark ride.

We figured that after all of those rides, our mothers would be gaining on us so we should hide out in the Fun in the Dark ride. We assumed, of course, this would be a great way to lose our mothers. From there we would next race down to where the sea lion exhibit was and, after watching the sea lion act, we would then board the train for a trip around the park. Judy and I felt we had devised the master plan. We wouldn't have to be bothered with tag along brother and sister.

Well, like all good plans, ours ran amuck. Judy and I did get to ride on the jack rabbit and the octopus. We were so proud of ourselves for making such a fast and great escape. Our mothers, however, seemed to always be one step ahead of us, and not the least bit pleased with our immature behavior. To our great dismay, when we got off the Octopus ride, both of them were there to greet us.

I will never forget the shock and the horror that Judy and I experienced on that hot August day. How could they have caught up with us so quickly? How did they know where we would be? We hadn't shared our game plan with any one. One thing was for sure - we knew by the expressions on their faces that we were in deep trouble. Immediately, we were questioned about our childish reasoning for doing such a dumb thing. They asked to see how many tickets we had left. We tried to explain that we each had only used six tickets. We offered our apologies, and said we would never ever do such a stupid thing again.

Mom and Aunt Mary accepted our apologies, took the remaining tickets and divided them between Jane, Richard, and Janice. Judy and I couldn't believe what we were seeing! Our younger siblings were now getting our tickets! This was absolutely horrific! To make matters even worse, our mothers made us stand by their sides for the remainder of the day and watch each and every ride Janice, Jane and Richard rode. The pain for Judy and me was too great! Tears began to well up in our eyes and within a few seconds the loud sobs commenced.

How could our mothers be so mean to us? This was not fair! To add to our remorse and dismay, Mom bought additional tickets for Richard, Jane and Janice. No one will ever know the pain and the anguish that Judy and I suffered that day. When the day came to an end, Judy and I could hardly wait to get into the car and head for home. Our hearts were broken.

The only lecture that Judy and I received that day stemmed from the Sunday School stories that Mom and Aunt Mary taught: "when we confess our sins there is forgiveness; however, when we sin, there is punishment." The memories of that embarrassing moment, coupled with the love and the forgiveness that came from my mother, will remain with me always. Two wise mothers – two foolish daughters!

ROMANCE AND
THE MAGIC CAROUSEL

As a child, I loved to ride the most magnificent and magical carousel in the whole world. I am referring to the Looff Carousel, which made its home in Spokane, almost 100 years ago.

I am not sure if it was the thrill of being able to ride on a pretend Trojan-like horse which had the longest and thickest tail, and was adorned with an abundance of sumptuous rubies, emeralds and sapphire jewels. Maybe it was the excitement of riding on the backs of the palominos, black stallions and white lighting horses that were adorned with exotic flowers and cherubs. Possibly it was the thrill of the Merry – Go – Round going so fast, while the horse kept going up and down and let me pretend I was racing my own horse.

The carousel was adorned in a glitter of bright lights. These were reflected in huge panel mirrors that hung in the center of the merry – go - round. To add to the romance and excitement, the German-made Adolphe Ruth & Sohn organ with its 300 pipes played John Philip Sousa marching music.

For my brother Richard, it was the excitement of grabbing the gold rings as he whizzed by the ring machine. A gold ring meant a free ride; twelve silver rings also meant a free ride. The problem, of course, was being able to quickly grab those rings as the merry – go –round raced past the ring machine. The ring machine had this long extended arm that contained an open slot for metal rings to slide into. The rings were larger than a fifty cent piece and were made out of metal. The platform that held this arm was 12 feet away from the carousel and stood about 13 feet off the ground.

Opposite the ring machine on a far wall was a giant size clown's face. The mouth of the clown was wide open. After grabbing a ring, we tried tossing it into the clown's open mouth as the carousel quickly whizzed by.

When riding on the Carousel, I would pretend I was riding my favorite horse in Spokane's Lilac Parade while accompanying one of the high school bands. It was exhilarating and electrifying fun. Glaring lights shot beams of bright rays around the entire carousel. As my palomino stallion was going up and down, I could hear the drum beat of the marching Sousa music, while seeing my reflection in the gigantic mirrors.

It was fun to listen to my grandparents tell stories about their youth, and how thrilling it was to go to Natatorium Park and ride on the popular Looff Carousel. Grandma Schafer loved to recite how she and grandpa spent much of their courtship riding on this elegant merry –go –round. On one occasion, while they were riding the Looff Carousel, grandpa Schafer proposed to grandma. It was a warm summer evening, and grandpa insisted that he and grandma sit on the bright red two-seater benches that had lavishly carved black dragon on each end. Grandpa had given a tip to the man who was operating the carousel ride and asked him to make the carousel ride last twice as long so he could propose to grandma. Ruby Doyen accepted Ben Schafer's proposal of marriage. They were married in June 1914.

According to Grandpa Schafer, The Looff Carousel was built between 1907 and 1909 by a German, Charles Looff who came to America when he was in his late teens. In his spare time while working at a furniture factory, he would carve wooden animals. As he created these elegant animals, he gave some of them to his children.

The carousel that has long been in Spokane was originally intended to be a wedding gift for his daughter Emma. In newspaper articles written by The Spokesman- Review, in 1907, Charles was asked by the Washington Water Power Company to build a carousel for Natatorium Park. When his work was completed, he notified Washington Water Power the price was $20,000. Washington Water Power complained about the hefty price tag. According to The Spokesman-Review, Charles struck a deal with the water power company: "If they allowed his son-in-law, Louis Vogel, to operate the carousel and other park concessions on a percentage basis, Looff would ship the carousel to Natatorium Park. The power company agreed, and on July 18, 1909, the carousel horses made their first revolutions in Spokane."

Natatorium Park flourished under Louis Vogel's management. He attracted big name performers and purchased new rides for the park. It was said that almost 100,000 people rode on the Looff Carousel every year.

A SIDE NOTE.

Today this marvelous, magical, and magnificent carousel graces Spokane's Riverfront Park and is one of the most popular rides and attractions. From Spokane Street to Main Street and throughout the park, one can hear the Looff Carousel and the German-made organ echoing the sounds of several marching bands, stirring the hearts and souls of little children and young lovers, while bringing back precious memories to parents, grandparents, great grandparents and most of all, me and my family.

THE ALLERS FAMILY

It was in late 1954 that Howard and Delores Allers purchased a piece of property on 22nd Street near Browne. Howard was working as a contractor and very busy building homes throughout Spokane County. His family had outgrown the first home that he built on the south side of Spokane on Perry near the Golf Course.

The house on 22nd Street would be the second home that Howard would soon begin building for his expanding family. In the fall of 1955, Howard, with his wife Delores and their five children, Arlene, the twins Jackie and Judy, Jim and Nick, moved into the new-two story home with attached garage and basement.

Mom and Dad were thrilled to welcome this new family into the neighborhood. It wasn't, however, until the Allers family actually moved into the house that Mom and Dad realized how much in common they had with this lively and vivacious couple. Both couples had war stories and memories of growing up in Spokane to share with one another.

Delores Allers, like Dorothy Magney, had been born and raised in Spokane. She grew up in a one story home on 18th near Manito Park with her older sister, Beatrice, and her younger sister Patricia. Her parents were strong Irish Catholics who attended St. Augustine Parish. Her father began his working career as a young man working for the Spokane Police Department. In 1948, when he retired, he held the rank of Captain.

When Delores graduated from Marycliff High School, she went to work at the Montgomery Ward department store in the heart of downtown Spokane. Delores was earning twelve dollars a week while working at the department store Monday through Saturday. By today's standards, twelve dollars seems like nothing. But in those days, one was grateful to have a job, and a young person could make twelve dollars go a long way. Like most single women in the 40s, Delores lived at home with her parents.

One evening when Delores and her girl friends got off work, they decided to drive out to Felts Field and have dinner at the Felts Field Coffee Shop. Felts Field was used as a small airport and training area for new pilots. This was a good opportunity for Delores and her companions to meet the guys and enjoy a meal. It was a means of entertainment.

Delores is a charmer and a talker with personality plus. She is a tall brunette with stunning big round chocolate brown eyes. Like most Irish folks, she did not have a bashful bone in her body. Meeting strangers and starting up a conversation always came easy for Delores. That evening at the Coffee Shop, Delores meet a handsome and charming Army Air Force Officer, Lieutenant Howard Allers, who had just finished instructing a group of pilots in the technique of night flying.

After graduating from college with a degree in education and industrial arts, Howard joined the Armed Forces. He was sent to Spokane to teach night flying at Felts Field.

Howard had a passion for working with his hands and building furniture. Like his father, grandfather and great grandfather, Howard was a master craftsman with a piece of wood and could build anything.

Delores was also talented. Her love and passion was sewing and making clothes for her sisters and friends. One of her favorite past times was to visit fabric stores, study patterns and look for the newest fabrics.

While eating dinner at the Felts Field Coffee Shop, Howard and Delores struck up a conversation. The next day, Howard dressed in his military uniform, waited for Delores to get off work so he could invite her out for dinner. Howard approached Delores as she was exiting the department store. Flattered but somewhat surprised, she accepted his invitation and said she would be honored. First, however, she needed to go home and change her clothes, and introduce Howard to her parents. What she wanted to say, but didn't and

145

couldn't, was, "I can go out to dinner with you if my parents approve." Delores' parents took an immediate liking to Howard. Prior to meeting Howard, her father had very negative opinions about the young men serving in the military. Delores was uncertain if her father would allow her to go on a date with an army officer. Howard was very much like Delores, full of charm and personality. When Delores introduced Howard to her parents, they were mesmerized with his "military spit and polish."

The young couple dated for seven months before Howard proposed marriage. They were married on February 7, 1942 at St. Augustines Parish.

In April 1942, Howard was sent to Columbia, South Carolina, and Eglin Field near Pensacola, Florida, to train on the two engine, B-25 Billy Mitchell bomber. Delores remained in Spokane, but was able to visit him on several different occasions. His last station of duty would be China.

The 17th Bomber Group that Howard belonged to supplied the aircraft and aircrew for the famous Lt. Colonel Jimmie Doolittle-led air raid on Tokyo on April 18, 1942. The raid didn't cause much damage, but was a great morale builder for the country after the string of defeats the United States suffered at the hands of the Japanese, beginning with the attack on Pearl Harbor on December 7, 1941. The Doolittle-led raid was also famous because the attacking B-25 bombers took-off from the aircraft carrier U.S.S. Hornet. The B-25 bomber was not designed to operate from an aircraft carrier, and this raid was the first, and last time, they did. The puzzled Japanese government didn't know where the bombers came from. President Roosevelt announced that they flew from Shangra-La, the mythical kingdom in the Himalayas.

The 17th Bomber Group, equipped with B-25 Mitchell bombers, was sent to the 14th U.S. Army Air Force in China in mid 1942. B-25 pilot, Lieutenant Howard Allers, found himself in China flying bombing missions against the Japanese.

On October 25, 1942, Lt. Allers took part in the largest bombing mission against the Japanese in China to date. Ten B-25 bombers, escorted by 7 P-40 Warhawk fighter planes, took-off from Kweilin Field around 9:00 A.M. and headed for Japanese shipping in Victoria Harbor and the docks at Hong

Kong and Kowloon. After the bomb run, Lt. Allers B-25 was hit by anti-aircraft fire and an engine was disabled. Slowed by flying on one engine and lagging behind the rest of the formation, his bomber was attacked by Japanese twin-engined fighters. One of the Japanese fighters shot his bomber to pieces and shot him in the foot. Two of the bomber crew bailed out and were captured immediately. Even though wounded, Lt. Allers managed to crash land his plane and destroy the Norden Bombsight, which was still a secret to the enemy. The two crew members who stayed with the plane carried him clear of the plane and bandaged his foot.

Lt. Allers begged them to leave him alone and escape. They refused to go without him. While traveling through Japanese lines that night, the three of them stopped to rest. In the dark, Howard crawled away from his two crew mates to give them a better chance to escape from the Japanese, which eventually they were able to do. Lt. Allers was captured by the Japanese and placed in a hospital until he recovered from his wounded foot. At that point, he was then placed in aprisoner-of-war camp for the next three years until the Japanese surrendered in mid-August 1945.

The bombing mission in which Howard was shot down, and his exploits once he was on the ground, is memorialized in Colonel Robert L. Scott Jr's book "God Is My Co-Pilot." Colonel Scott commanded the fighter escort on this mission.

It was not until the first of November that Delores received word that Howard was missing in action. Later, she received word from the military that he was a prisoner of war.

To keep herself busy and help support the troops during this tragic time in her newly married life, Delores went to work at the Post Exchange at Galene Field. Today, this base is called Fairchild Air Force Base. While Howard remained a prisoner of war, she received two brief letters from him. Then, in October, 1945, during a World Series game, Delores received exciting news about the release of her husband from a Japanese prisoner-of-war camp. When Captain Allers was released from the camp, he received the Purple Heart, the Distinguished Flying Cross, and the Silver Star medals.

Following Howard's release, he returned to Spokane and Delores. Due to the serious injuries he suffered to his foot when his plane was shot down Howard had to undergo numerous surgeries, and for many months had to wear a cast on his foot.

While recuperating from his foot surgeries, Howard and Delores purchased four and half acres of land on Perry near the golf course. As soon as he was able, he went to work building a new home for his young family. Delores was expecting her first child, Arlene, who was born in September of 1946. When Arlene was seven months old, Delores became pregnant and delivered a set of twin girls on December 1, 1947, named Jackie and Judy. By the time Arlene was ready to start school, Howard and Delores realized they located in an area on the south hill where there were no schools. This became the motivating factor for them to sell the home and property. They purchased a home on 17th , where Arlene and the twins attended Lincoln Heights Elementary School.

Finding work in Spokane was easy for Howard. Building materials were plentiful, and most of the returning GI's were purchasing new homes for their families. Because Howard was a master craftsman, it was only natural that he would find himself in demand constructing homes for others and his own young growing family. While Howard was constructing houses, School District 81 discovered that Howard had a bachelor's degree in education, and was certified to teach. At that time, the school district was struggling to find industrial arts teachers for the local high schools. He was approached by the school district and offered a job teaching industrial arts at Lewis and Clark High School. Realizing the good benefits that come with teaching and the opportunity to use his college education, Howard eventually decided to accept the offer.

Eric was one of the first neighbors to introduce himself to the new Allers family. One morning when the Allers had been in the house for a couple of weeks, the door bell rang. Delores went to open the front door. There stood a giant of a man wanting to know if she had some "Axs." Delores was puzzled. She didn't know what "Axs" meant. Delores apologized, and said she didn't know what "Axs" meant. Eric then apologized for his broken English and thick Dutch accent, and said he needed a dozen "Axs" (eggs.) Delores got Eric his dozen "Axs," and a new immediate friendship was born.

Shortly after the Allers family moved into the neighborhood, Mom was planning on hosting a big neighborhood gathering. However, I became violently ill with the dreaded disease known as MUMPS. When Delores heard the news, she volunteered to have the party at their home. Eric said he would assist Delores and supply the appetizers and some wine. Dad made a brief appearance, and then came back home to help Mom play doctor. The night of the party was the first time that Delores and Howard met Erna Bert and the other neighbors.

The five Allers children helped to entertain the guests by having a talent show. Eric and Erna Bert acted as the judges. Needless to say, this fun and vivacious new family on 22nd Street made a lasting impression on all the neighbors.

There is no wonder why this innovative family became quickly loved by everyone on our short little street. New to the area with five young children, they were willing to open up their home and hearts to strangers while helping out a fellow neighbor. This life style for the Allers family never changed. The Allers were always the first family to come to the aid of friends and neighbors. They had the strength and capacity to set aside their own problems, and put the needs of others first. Their generosity extended to any one who was down on his or her luck and misfortune. Delores was always baking cakes and making flower arrangements for neighbors and friends. Howard was always playing the role of the delivery man. The two were a dynamic duo whose energy and talents amazed everyone.

SEVERAL SIDE NOTES.

In the sixties when I was attending Lewis and Clark High School, Howard was the person who provided my transportation to school. He owned a big swept-wing station wagon. Arlene, Jackie and Judy, twin nephews Dick and Bobby Brown, Lija Zilgme, myself, and once in a while someone else, would pile into the car at 7:00 A.M. and head to school.

When he retired from teaching, he did not retire from life. He began a business building grandfather clocks. Howard's clocks were the most gorgeous clocks I have ever seen. People from all over the states and Europe came to Spokane to purchase his one-of-a-kind, grandfather clocks.

While Howard was building his clocks, Delores decided to take up oil painting and quickly discovered she had a flare with the paint brush. Today, her magnificent floral paintings can be seen throughout her house and in the homes of friends and relatives.

In the 60s, Mom and Delores combined their cooking talents and formed a catering business known as D&D Catering. The business was extremely successful and lasted until my mother had to have serious foot surgery. During the years of the catering business, all of the Magney and Allers kids worked in the business. We found ourselves immediately drafted when one of the hired waiters or dishwashers could not make it to work. This happened quite regularly. While the kids found themselves washing dishes, setting up tables, pouring coffee and even cooking, Dad and Howard were the delivery experts, carting hot and cold food all over the city of Spokane.

The Allers Family
Left to right: Howard Allers, Nick, Arlene, Delores Allers, and Jim.
Back row: twins Judy and Jackie. Photo take in 1958 by Erna Bert Nelson.

ACCORDION MOMENTS

The early 1950's offered one of the most exciting times to be a child, or so I thought at the time. A great new invention was sweeping the country. In the mind of a young person who was seven years old, this invention was the wonders of wonders!

Our family would sit in front of a wooden box that had a glass front. Beneath the glass front was a row of round knobs that actually turned. By turning one of the round knobs to the right or the left, a picture would appear or disappear on the glass screen. Another dial made the picture fuzzy, clear or look like a line of ribbons. There was a knob which made the picture very dark, bright or clear.

The pictures on this glass screen were always black, white or neutral gray. The most amazing thing about the picture was that it contained people who would move and talk. What a wonderful thing it was!

Today, of, course, we call all that walking and talking simply "programs." One of the most popular TV programs of the 50's was the Lawrence Welk show. Every Saturday night at 8 o'clock, it became a family ritual for the family to gather in front of the TV to be entertained by Lawrence Welk and his Champagne Music Makers.

Richard and I were bathed and in our pajamas, ready for bed. Bedtime really was 8 o'clock, but on Saturday nights, we were allowed to stay up until 9 in order to watch this oh-so-special show.

At 9 o'clock, we knew it was time to roll into bed without any thought of asking for a drink of water or pretending we were not sleepy. It was such a special treat, we were not about to risk losing it by arguing at bedtime.

One of Mom and Dads favorites on the Welk show was Myron Floren. He was an accordion wizard. On some occasions Mr. Welk would pick up his own accordion and together they would play a duet. In my mother's eyes, Myron was the most talented person she had ever seen.

I am not sure if the accordion popularity was nation wide, state wide, city wide or strictly unique to 22nd street. Regardless, it was not just the Magney family who sang the praises of the musical show and the talented Myron Floren, it was the entire neighborhood.

At the Aller's house, this was also the special event for Saturday night. At either the Magney or the Allers household, we could anticipate that Eric would be joining our families.

The Saturday night ritual lasted for several years. Both Dorothy and Delores decided, however, that there was more to be done during the hour than simply sitting and watching this fun musical program. The two mothers believed there was musical talent in their offspring and it was imperative to quickly begin developing and training their children's musical gifts.

Mom believed that I did not have much of an aptitude for music and I would benefit more by singing in the kid's church choir.

Richard had a much better singing voice. Because I was taking dancing lessons and singing in the church choir, I managed to escape taking accordion lessons. The Aller twins, Judy and Jackie, showed absolutely no interest in music or the accordion. Howard and Delores believed that Arlene showed the most musical promise in their family. Eventually, it was Arlene and Richard who were destined to fulfill their mothers' musical ambitions.

Mom and Delores knew a Spokane gentleman who played (they believed) the accordion better than Myron Floren. His name was Mr. Ilmar Kuljus. Both refugees from Estonia, Ilmar and his wife Dolly, were well-educated and well known in their homeland for their musical and artistic talents.

Mr. Kuljus was a tall, slender, handsome man whose long slender fingers were quick and nimble. His fingers could race across the key board with great speed and dexterity. His polka songs were happy and quick, and he could entertain everyone with the most popular songs of the day.

At the time that Delores decided to start Arlene with accordion lessons, Ilmar Kuljus had a full load of students. Dolores discovered another accordion instructor, Mr. Attwood, who had room for new students. She enrolled Arlene in his classes. Arlene's lessons continued for about two years with Mr. Attwood.

Eventually, Mom decided she had wasted time by not getting Richard started with lessons. She, however, had her heart set on Richard having accordion lessons only with Ilmar Kuljus. A phone call was placed to Ilmar. Mom went into great detail explaining how her nine year old son was gifted musically and the only person who was qualified to work and develop Richard's talents would be Mr. Kuljus.

Mom's persuasion worked, and somehow Ilmar found time to teach Richard. Shortly after Richard started his accordion lessons, Mom phoned Delores to say that she had been able to enroll Richard in private lessons at home with Mr. Kuljus.

Dolores then phoned Ilmar, and explained that Arlene had been taking lessons with another person, but she really believed he could improve Arlene's accordion skills. She was hoping he could find time to give Arlene private lessons at their home. Mr. Kuljus graciously rearranged his hectic accordion schedule and added Arlene to his student roster.

In the eyes of Dolores and Dorothy, Arlene and Richard were two of the luckiest kids in Spokane, Washington. They were having the "opportunity of a life time." Richard and Arlene would be studying the accordion and learning it from none other than a great master.

Arlene and Richard, however, were neither thrilled nor happy about this decision. Richard did not like, nor did he want to play, the accordion. Arlene also disliked the big boxy instrument. Practice time was not a fun time at either home. In fact, on some occasions, it became a yelling match in both households.

At first, the lessons for Arlene and Richard were private. Arlene was more advanced than Richard, and had graduated from playing the "baby accordion" to using the "big red accordion." Mr. Kuljus would come to the Magney home, patiently teaching Richard for 45 minutes. These were some of the longest 45 minutes in Richard's life. At the conclusion of those lessons, Mr. Kuljus would pack up his Myron Floren size accordion and walk to the Allers home to instruct Arlene. The accordion ritual continued for more than a year, much to the chagrin of Richard and Arlene.

After a year of private lessons for Richard, it was time for him to advance up to the "big accordion." Richard, however, tried to persuade our parents he was ready to discontinue playing the accordion. He informed Mom and Dad he preferred to spend more time in the "club house" with his neighborhood buddies, Jim Hawley and Mike Pearson. As far as he was concerned he wanted to forget there was such a thing as a "squeeze box." Mom and Dad held firm. They believed learning to master the accordion was a more productive way for a young boy to spend his time.

Richard, however, refused to have a red accordion like Arlene. He was not about to look like "a girl." Heaven forbid! Richard settled for the black accordion which came with a huge case that was lined in a bright red crushed velvet material.

In addition to this joyous moment for Richard and the Magney household, Mr. Kuljus recommended to both sets of parents that the time had come for both Arlene and Richard to now participate in weekly group lessons.

The two accordion prodigies had graduated from private lessons to group classes. How fortunate can one get! To add to the excitement of being in the accordion band, these lessons would be on Saturday, the most precious day of the week for kids and their chums. Richard played in the accordion band for about three years and Arlene until she was seventeen. Both, absolutely hating the experience!! Richard had less time to spend with his buddies. Arlene was always affected with stage fright, and as a young teen, she felt she had no social life with her girl friends.

The grand acclaim to all of these lessons always climaxed with The Recital. Most of 22nd Street was well represented when Recital time came around. Friends of Mr. Kuljus were also friends of the Magneys and the Allers.

Therefore, one could always count on a super attendance for these monumental occasions.

Behind the scenes, however, was another story. Richard hated the accordion. He liked Mr. Kuljus who was most patient and professional. A real tug-of-war ensued with mother and son. Dorothy was adamant that her son Richard would learn to play the accordion. Richard rebelled by refusing to practice. Consequently, before most lessons began, there were numerous arguments at the Magney house. After four years of this tug of war game, Richard finally won the battle and was given permission to discontinue the accordion lessons.

This was one of Dorothy's heartbreaks. She just absolutely knew her son was destined to become the next Myron Floren. Mom truly believed, that in time, Richard would return to playing the accordion. Dorothy never gave up on that dream.

The accordion scenario was much the same at the Allers household as it was at the Magney home. Arlene didn't dislike the accordion as much as she resented her mother instructing her on how to play the instrument. Dolores had lots of musical talent, and played the organ splendidly. She had an ear for music, and also had visions of her daughter becoming the female Myron Floren. Even though Arlene had an ear for music, she found reading music difficult, especially as the songs were becoming more complicated. Arlene never shared her parents' ambition. And so a weekly tug of war also occurred at the Allers home. Arlene's struggle lasted much longer than Richard's. She continued with the lessons until she was 17. At that point she told her parents that she was "through with the accordion."

SEVERAL SIDE NOTES.

Arlene received her first pair of high heeled shoes for one of the band recitals. Dolores was insistent that Arlene look professional and dressy. Arlene, on the other hand was embarrassed to wear the shoes. She was only fourteen and not impressed with dressing up.

Years later, when Arlene's father, Howard, was in the hospital, dying with cancer; he asked her if she still had the accordion. Arlene said, "Yes, she did, but she did not play it any more." Howard told her, to always keep it. He had paid a lot of money for it and maybe some day she would play it again.

Dorothy Magney refused to sell or give away Richard's accordion. In her

155

heart, she knew one day Richard would open the carrying case, strap that accordion to his shoulders and play the instrument. Unfortunately, the accordion remained in the basement of Dorothy's home for years, packed away in the red velvet lined case. When Dorothy went to live with Marilyn, the cumbersome accordion case accompanied Dorothy to my home where it remained tucked away in the basement. In all those years that followed, Richard never wanted anything to do with that blooming black instrument, and he never touched the case again in his life.

Richard Magney and his famous accordion.
Pictured with Richard is his younger sister, Janice.

THE ZILGMES

One of the homes on 22nd Street belonged to Edmunds and Irene Zilgme. The home the Zilgmes lived in was not a new home like those of the Allers and the Magney homes. The Zilgme's house was built around 1917 and was one of the first homes built on 22nd Street. An elderly couple by the name of Berley were the original owners. They raised their family in this old house, and remained in the home until they passed away in the mid fifties. The home was typical of the homes built in the era of 1917: one bathroom, two bedrooms, tiny kitchen and an unattached garage that was located at the back of the house. Upstairs, there was a large attic, big enough to accommodate another bedroom or become a giant size play room.

The most wonderful feature about this old home was the marvelous front porch with dimensions of 10x14. To afford privacy to those sitting on the porch, there was a wooden railing that stood two and a half feet high and enclosed the front porch.

Their older daughter, Lija, became one of my closest friends. Her parents were refugees from Latvia. During World War II, when the Russians invaded the Baltic countries, Edmunds and Irene fled to Germany. Irene was a registered nurse and was able to support the family by working as a nurse in a displaced persons camp. It was at this camp that Lija was born in February of 1947. The camp was to become the home of Edmunds and Irene until they received a sponsorship from the Lutheran Church to come to the United States. The Zilgmes were given the opportunity to select the city in the US where they preferred to live. Following numerous discussions with family and

157

friends who were already residing in America, they decided Dallas, Texas, would be the best place for them to make their new home. Lija had tuberculosis, and doctors advised Irene and Edmunds to select a city that would have warm temperatures and mild winters. Edmunds had brothers who resettled in New York. His brothers strongly encouraged Edmunds to bring his family to the largest city in the US, where the best doctors in the world could be found to take care of Lija. Because New York winters are cold and harsh, a tough decision was reached. They would not move to New York.

They did, however, have some friends and a few relatives who were living in Dallas. These Latvian friends strongly encouraged them to select Dallas, Texas, due to the wonderful climatic conditions that would be of benefit to Lija. Edmunds and Irene were assured that Lija could be successfully treated in Texas for TB by wonderful and caring physicians.

Edmunds, Irene and Lija made the trip to America by ship when Lija was two and half years old. Their port of entry was New Orleans. Irene recalls that she was very disappointed when she saw the Mississippi River for the first time. Because of all the wonderful songs she heard about the Mississippi, she assumed the river would be massive in size and the water would be a clear or vibrant blue color. Instead, she discovered the mighty Mississippi River was very narrow is some areas, filled with sandbars, and the water was murky and grey. It was difficult for her to understand why Americans had such a love for this dirty old river.

The Zilgmes lived and worked on a farm in Dallas for several years. Edmunds, who had been raised as a city boy was an attorney in Latvia, and was now working as a farm hand. He did not share Irene's love for their big new city with lots of stores for shopping. Irene, also, found herself working on the farm milking cows, something she had never before done in her life!

The young refugee family was paid sixty dollars a month to work virtually as slaves. With sixty dollars, they had to pay all their own living expenses. While the weather was wonderful, there came a point when they believed they were being taken advantage of by their American sponsors.

Irene's dearest friend from Latvia, Gunna Gustvas, had found sponsorship in Spokane, Washington. Gunna understood the miserable conditions Irene and Edmunds were living under. Out of love and concern, she encouraged the Zilgme's to consider relocating to Spokane.

Numerous Latvian friends residing in Spokane believed it would be easy for Edmunds to find employment at the Kaiser Aluminum plant in Trentwood. Irene, with her nursing skills could work at one of the local hospitals as a nurse. The Zilgmes were assured Spokane had a marvelous medical community, and excellent doctors could be found to provide for Lija's medical needs.

When Lija was five and half years old and Irene was six months pregnant with their second child Karina, the Zilgme family moved to Spokane.

For several years, they rented a little house on 17th near Thor and Freya. The home was owned by some of their Latvian friends. During the few years they lived in the rental home, the Zilmes became good friends with their American neighbors, the Burroughs family. Irene developed a close friendship with Phyliss Burroughs who had several children. Linda, was the oldest, next was a son Randy, Lija's age, and the youngest child was baby brother, Timmy.

Another family who was living on 17th at that time was Howard and Delores Allers.

When Lija started school at Lincoln Heights Elementary with Randy, she could not speak a word of English. A classmate, Arlene Allers, one day commented to her mother that she felt sorry for the new student in her class. Arlene explained to her mother that the little girl could not speak. Delores first thought her daughter meant the new student might be deaf, and it was not until a few years later, when the Allers and the Zilgmes moved into their homes on 22nd Street (about September 1955), that Delores Allers realized that Arlene meant the

Lija and Karina Zilgme in the Magney's backyard on 22nd Street.

159

child, could not speak a word of English.

In January 1953, Irene gave birth to a beautiful brown-eyed daughter that was named Karina. Irene and Edmunds continued to live in their rental home until Karina was more than two years old. By then, it became apparent that a larger house was necessary for this growing family. It was also at this time that they learned their rental house was going up for sale, and they would need to find another place to live.

It was at this juncture of their lives that a decision was made to purchase a home in Spokane. The old Berley home on 22nd Street had been on the market for quite some time when the Zilgmes made an offer that was accepted. According to Irene, when they first moved into the house it was in deplorable condition. Some of the kitchen drawers would not open, faucets were not working, the basement was bare and empty, and the upstairs had not been finished into another bedroom or a playroom.

I do not remember the exact day the Zilgmes moved into their new home. I do recall Mom and another neighbor lady, Alene Weeks, delivering food to Irene and Edmonds and welcoming them to the neighborhood. I was thrilled to discover the Zilgme's had a daughter my age. The first time I met Lija was at her home. It was also my first experience with hearing someone my age speak a foreign language. I took it for granted that when I heard my two grandfathers speaking German and Swedish, it was only the elderly who communicated in a foreign tongue. More amazing was to eventually learn that the Zilgmes spoke four languages. Besides Latvian, they were fluent in German, Russian and Polish. Now they were tackling the English language. A remarkable family had moved onto 22nd Street!

SEVERAL SIDE NOTES:

Even though the Zilgme family moved to a new house on a different part of the South Hill, Irene and Phyliss Burroughs continued their friendship for many years. Lija introduced me to Randy one day when I went to see if Lija wanted to go swimming. Randy and I became good friends.

When I was about 18 or 19, Randy joined the Coast Guard. While he was gone for a few days, I was given the responsibility to take good care of his little

European sports car. I don't think I ever shared this with Randy, but Lija and I managed to have a great time with his little English sports car. We took the little two-seater for several hot spins around town on various warm summer evenings. We referred to this fun as "tooling town."

Today Irene and Edmunds Zilgme still remain in the old Berley house. Their original intentions were to fix up the home and then sell it. Remodel and fix it up they did. The old attic was made into a beautiful play room, and the ugly old basement was refinished with brick and a wet bar. The antiquated kitchen with the faucets that didn't work, and drawers that wouldn't open, were all replaced. They transformed the home on 22nd Street, into a place of warmth and comfort where friends loved to gather.

PAPER DOLLS

Summer time in Spokane, especially in July or August, could be extremely hot. Spokane is located east of the Cascade Mountains and is almost 260 miles inland from the Pacific Ocean. The climate in Spokane is always dry. Summers are hot and dry and winter months are cold and arid. Rain and moisture must climb over the Cascade Range of mountains with an elevations of 4000 to more than 14,000 feet, Mt. Rainer being the highest. The average summer temperature may vary from a comfortable 78 degrees to a blistering 105. One of the marvelous features of the climate is that most nights, the temperature drops to the high 50's. This means the average family can get a good night's sleep, and wake refreshed and ready to start the next day with plenty of energy.

On those hot summer days, Lija Zilgme, and me, could be seen sitting on the Zilgme's front porch, playing with our "paper dolls."

Like the cowboy and Indian toys for little boys, paper dolls were a very popular toy for young girls in the fifties and provided a very inexpensive means of entertainment. During the fifties in Spokane, there were no big Toy's R US stores. There was, however, the Crescent Department Store, a Bon Marche and my favorite, Kress, a super five- and-dime store that was located directly across the street from the Crescent on Main Street. Woolworth's had a large store west of Kress. On Riverside, east of the Crescent, was the popular Newberry store. Any of these stores along with a few family-owned drug stores, would carry a limited selection of paper dolls.

Part of the great fun in playing with paper dolls was the process of deciding which store to visit first and rummage through their collection. The purchase of a new set of paper dolls could take all day.

Lija and I lived for the moment our daily chores were completed and swimming or dancing lessons were finished. Spending time together on her front porch, and un-wrapping our new set of paper dolls to discover which set the other had chosen, was so exciting. Oh, for the love of those paper dolls.

For today's young readers who were born many years after the invention of paper dolls, I will do my best to describe what paper dolls resembled and how they were packaged. Most paper dolls came in sheets of paper. Some where displayed in a magazine format and stamped on to heavy glossy paper. Other paper doll collections were placed on light weight construction paper and were often packaged in boxes. Some sets resembled the famous Betsy Dolls that were popular in the fifties. Other paper doll sets would feature an entire family; mommy, daddy, brother, sister and the new baby. Some even included the grandparents. One of the most popular paper doll sets was the Lennon Sisters set. The Lennon sisters were four young sisters who were regular guests on the Lawrence Welk Saturday night TV program. The girls ranged in age from nine to fifteen. There harmony was almost perfect, and TV audiences adored these wholesome sisters.

Lija and I, however, were enthralled with what I believe was possibly the fore runner to Mattel's Barbie and Ken. Lija and I would only buy the "Wedding Paper Dolls." The typical package included the bride, bridesmaid, groom, best man and, once in awhile, there would be a flower girl and a ring bearer. The hardest part of selecting the perfect paper doll set was to first decided which brides dress was the most elegant, or which set had the most elaborate set of sophisticated clothing. The more expensive paper doll sets contained lavish wardrobes along with the flowers for the wedding party, candelabras sets and decorations for an outside wedding or a church wedding. These plush sets were usually packaged in puzzle size boxes because the dolls had to be punched out of the card-board construction. The clothes for the dolls were on glossy paper and had to be cut with scissors, very carefully.

Cutting out the clothes was time consuming, and became an art. There were little white strips of paper that were part of the outfits and were placed on the shoulders and the sides of the clothing. These strips were used to attach the clothing to the paper dolls. When cutting out the doll's clothing, it was important to cut the white strip so it remained attached to the article of clothing. If the white strip should be cut off (heaven forbid), the outfit could not be attached to the paper doll.

On those hot summer afternoons when Lija and I were nine, ten and eleven, we could be seen sitting on the Zilgme's front porch playing with our paper dolls. We were oblivious to the heat, or the time of day, or the world around us. For endless hours, we lived in our own little fantasy world, playing with our paper dolls.

Our usual format for playing paper dolls after all the cutting out of the clothing had occurred, was for each of us to take a separate corner on the porch and play with our own dolls. On some occasions, we would combine the two sets on the center floor near the steps.

By chance, I wonder if today's little girls ages, nine to eleven could be entertained by the magic of paper dolls. I suppose not. Today's little girls live for the thrill of buying the latest Barbie doll that hits the consumer shelves.

A SIDE NOTE

The friendship of Marilyn and Lija continued to grow and flourish for many years. When they out grew paper dolls, their interest changed to sports, and then to boys.

Today, there are no more paper dolls for Lija and Marilyn. They have all been tucked away into puzzle boxes. They are safely stored up in the old attic, where memories and good times of hot summer days in Spokane, sleep eternally.

DADDY BUILDS A BOMB SHELTER

It is difficult to describe, some 35 or 40 years later, exactly what the mind-set was during the Cold War. As citizens, we were at "war," and yet we were not. We were asked to take all kinds of precautions, including the building of bomb shelters, and yet we had no precise identifiable dangers to face.

Many families devised destination plans. Should there be an attack from Russia or another communist country, and the family becomes separated, everyone would know where to find each other in the hours or days or weeks ahead.

With a river running through the center of Spokane, most families on any given day could have members on both sides of the river. The most likely scenario would find the mother and the children on one side, and the father at work on the opposite side. Evacuation plans were numerous, with evacuees moving away from the city in many directions, depending on the situation.

Many families carried food and water in the trunks of their cars for months. First aid supplies, flashlights, batteries, blankets, extra clothing, baby formula, and matches were only a few of the items regarded as necessities in the trunk of the car. These items were checked regularly by someone in the family who made certain the emergency supplies were fresh.

Other families preferred to follow the suggestions that every home should have a bomb shelter. Plans were available. Advice was free, but the exact requirements were vague because the exact dangers were not known. Daily the radio stations carried stories about the possibility of war, the likely-hood the

Russians (then our enemy) had rockets aimed at every major city in the US. With Fairchild Air Force Base in our back yard, the idea of an attack in Spokane did not seem too remote. No one knew when the attack would happen, if it would occur, and what would be the results. It was a difficult and intimidating time in America's history.

When we moved into our home on 22nd Street, the Korean War had been in progress for a year. I overheard a conversation between Mom and Dad, discussing the possibility that Daddy might be called back into active duty with the army. He stood a good chance to see action in Korea. As time progressed, these discussions became more frequent. I began having terrible nightmares and could not fathom the thought of my father leaving us to go off to war, wherever that might be. God did answer my prayers, and my father was not sent to Korea. Fortunately, his entire National Guard Unit remained in Spokane.

Dad was working as a full-time duty officer at the National Guard Armory in downtown Spokane on 202 West Second. This Armory building was constructed in 1908 and had a barn like interior. The Armory was used as the regional location for draft registration. Before Spokane built its Coliseum in 1954 the Armory was utilized by the high schools and colleges for athletic games and numerous civic events. The official purpose was to provide a place for drill practice for the different National Guard units. According to Dad, the holiday season was when the building was the busiest. During the Christmas season, the Armory was used by the post office for handling extra incoming letters and packages.

Dad's responsibility with the National Guard dictated that he work closely with the Civil Defense Department. He helped plan weekly air raid siren drills, organize evacuation routes, and assist with the planning of Spokane's "Operation Walkout." According to dad, who now held the rank of a Captain, if the US were to see war occur on its own soil, it was very probable nuclear attacks would be made against major cities. Spokane, because of its location, importance to transportation, and production of critical materials such as aluminum, could be among the first to be hit. "Operation Walkout" was aimed at preparing its citizens for such a disaster.

Dad took his duties as a father and protector very seriously. He was willing to fight the next battle to defend his country, save his city from attack, and shelter his family and friends from nuclear fall out. It was fall-out from nuclear attack that daddy became adamant about. It became his obsession.

He began talking about the importance and the necessity of building a bomb shelter in our home. He would come home at night and study numerous designs, and the effectiveness of each one. He became an expert on the various types and styles being built.

He didn't believe the designs of many of the shelter plans were sufficient to afford good protection. Mom and Dad spent hours researching shelter plans offered by Civil Defense officials.

One of the least expensive options cost about $125. That plan would hold four people and occupy one corner of the basement. Another shelter idea showed a prefab backyard shelter that would hold four people. The cost for the plan was $150, and included steel pipe for air vents.

There was the sand-filled lean-to shelter that would accommodate three people. This was the cheapest of the plans. Dad would tease me and say he was going to build a sand house for us kids to live in.

The last plan my parents analyzed in great depth was the most expensive, and consisted of building a basement compact shelter of sand filled concrete blocks. Solid blocks would be used on the roof.

There was, however, one big obstacle. The cost of this shelter plan was far greater than any of the previous plans they had studied. Even though Mom and Dad were comfortable financially, a Captain's income did place some financial limitations on the Magney household.

Dad approached Grandpa Magney and asked him if he would consider helping to finance the building of the bomb shelter. Grandpa was more than willing to do so.

The next step was to find a contractor who could draw blueprints, was qualified to build a shelter, and willing to work for what Mom and Dad would pay. Mom was adamant that she wanted the project to begin as soon as the ground was free of ice and no later than Mothers Day.

Just before construction was to begin, Mom and Dad made another home

Magney house on 22nd Street where the bomb shelter was built.

improvement decision; they would enlarge the basement, increase the size of the shelter, and expand the kitchen. The bomb shelter would now consist of at least two rooms. One would be for the storage of water, food, and other necessities, and the larger room would hold eight to twelve people. The entire shelter would be constructed with thick concrete blocks. Dad was an electrician and could install the wiring for lighting in the two rooms. Providing adequate ventilations was a major concern. It was critical for the safety of those who would reside in the shelter.

At last, the day arrived when the bull dozer and dump trucks were to show-up at our house. The first couple of days, neighbors came in droves to inspect the work in progress. Included in the wide range of guests were Grandma and Grandpa Magney, and Grandma and Grandpa Schafer. Eric came by at least once every day. He would often arrive at the house for breakfast and stay most of the day. Dick and Joan Eugene would stop by after working all day at the floral shop. Howard Allers made an appearance regularly to give advice and assist Dad with any new change or problems that arose.

Mom was constantly baking pies and cakes to serve to friends and family members who came to observe the progress.

That summer was not a fun time for me. Gone was our big green backyard. In its place were dirt, dust, and dump trucks.

This particular summer the weather was extra hot. Mom did not fare well in the heat. She was what I referred to as a yeller and a screamer. The one thing she hated more than the heat was dirt. This summer we had plenty of both, which left mom with a bad temperament and unhappy disposition.

Comstock Park was the only place that afforded me any real relief. The park provided a wonderful escape from the commotion that was taking place at home. The water in the Olympic size swimming pool was most refreshing, and the giant slide and swing sets allowed me to blow off steam.

After what seemed like an eternity of having our back yard torn up with construction equipment, the shelter project was finally completed.

A Side Note:

Like all major events on 22nd Street, whether it was a new beginning or a climatic ending, it meant one thing – it was time for a celebration. A party was planned. Family, friends and neighbors all congregated at the Magney house in honor of the bomb shelter. Dolores Allers assisted Mom.

She baked several of her super-size cakes that were beautifully decorated. She prepared a variety of salads for everyone to sample. Irene Zilgme made her famous Latvian peroges and furnished delicious cheeses. Eric cooked a big ham, and supplied the crowd with some of his favorite European wines. As always, the tables were overflowing with an abundance of wonderful food.

Looking back, I realize the Magney's bomb shelter really belonged to the entire neighborhood. I am probably wrong, but I doubt very much there was ever another bomb shelter built in Spokane that could rival the one on 22nd Street built by Jack and Dorothy Magney.

SPOKANE: A CITY OF RAILROAD LINES

Trains! Trains! Trains! They were all over Spokane, or so I thought. One of grandma Schafer's favorite places to park downtown was under the railroad tracks by the Union Railroad Station. It was such a grand experience to hear the train whistle, blow and toot. Each train's sound was unique. Some had large powerful engines that seemed to roar. Others had the smaller steam engines that pulled either smaller or fewer cars, and produced a lighter and slower chug, chug, chug sound. The trains that stopped in Spokane, (frequently referred to as the Inland Empire) transported both passengers and other shipments of all kinds. The most important freight trains in the 50s were ones that hauled grain from surrounding farming communities, where families made their living by growing wheat to feed the world. The railroad system made it possible for farmers to transport their agriculture products to either the East Coast or the West Coast.

Commuter trains were still very popular in the early 50s. Spokane did not have a large thriving airport. The average traveler or business man found using the train system provided a more convenient and least costly way to travel.

As a child, I thought it was a thrilling adventure to accompany my grandparents or parents downtown to the Union Railroad Station or the Great Northern Depot, to pick up packages or greet friends who were coming into Spokane.

Historical records show that the Great Northern Railroad was the first to lay track along the Spokane riverfront and Havermale Island, in 1901. This island is a small piece of land that sits in the Spokane River between Division

Street and Monroe Street. But it was in 1892 that the Great Northern railroad actually came to Spokane. James J. Hill built the Great Northern Railroad yard in the north east part of Spokane, known as the Hillyard switching yard. Many railroad men worked in this yard, including some of my ancestors. Over time, this area of Spokane became known as Hillyard.

The cost to build the Great Northern Depot in 1902 was $150,000. The Great Northern Building was a three- story tan brick structure that was trimmed with native sandstone. It faced the south channel of the Spokane River between Washington and Stevens streets. The tower portion of this three-story building contained four huge nine-foot (in diameter) clocks that graced each side of the tower. The waiting room for the train station had glossy white tiles, and rows and rows of dark wooden benches. A ticket office and baggage checking area were on the right side, an eating area and cigar/magazine counter on the left. The tracks were at ground level on the north side of the building. Between the building and the tracks were train sheds or covered areas that kept passengers protected from the outside elements. At one time in Spokane, the Great Northern Depot was one of the finest railroad depots west of Chicago.

According to my father, on July 4, 1881, the first Northern Pacific train came into Spokane. That train carried 6 boxcars loaded with passengers from Cheney. The Northern Pacific Depot was on Railroad Avenue. Railroad Avenue got its name because the railroad tracks went through the middle of the street. Several years later, the tracks were raised so cars could go underneath, and Railroad Avenue disappeared. The first trains from the east arrived in 1883, after the golden spike was driven at Helena, Montana.

Based on information acquired from Canfield and Wilders, *The Making of Modern American, and History of the United States Army*, by Russell Weigley, two important Federal Acts greatly impacted the development of the Pacific Northwest. The first was the Pacific Railway Act that President Lincoln signed into law in 1862. This law was the largest land grant act in the history of the United States. The law conditionally granted public lands for the purpose of connecting the east and west coasts by rail. Union Pacific and Central Pacific, chartered in that year, were the recipients of the land grant and connected the

East Coast to California. The Northern Pacific Railroad was chartered in 1864 to provide the link to the Pacific Northwest. The law provided over 155 million acres of public lands to the railroads for a right-of-way, and as a means of raising the capital to build and maintain the railroads. The land was granted in alternating square miles, creating a "checker-board" pattern of ownership. This pattern was intended to ensure that railroad access across the country would increase the value of those sections of land not granted to the railroad. Much of Spokane was included in the grant to Northern Pacific Railroad. The passage of the land grant was intended to open the vast resources of the West to the East.

The second important piece of legislation was The Homestead Act of 1862, which prompted more than 600,000 people to move west. This greatly impacted the West's economy and population. States, actually Territories at that time, like Washington, Idaho, and Montana, benefited from the Homestead Act through an increase in agriculture production, as well as, the huge population expansion. The Act went into effect on May 20th. A person could get 160 acres of land if they were a U.S. citizen and 21 years of age. They had to pay a filing fee of $10 and reside on the new farm in the West for at least five years. The land would then belong to them.

Information gathered from family stated that during the 1880s, there was a race going on to build railroads in the area between J.J. Browne, and Daniel Corbin. Browne was attempting to build a standard gauge railroad branching off from the Northern Pacific Railroad. His Railroad was to be connected by a steamboat sailing south down Coeur d'Alene Lake and then up the Coeur d'Alene River to a railroad line that would go to Wallace, Idaho. Mr. Browne mistakenly thought that in order to build the railroad, he had to get Congressional approval. A man named Daniel Corbin decided to copy J.J. Browne's plan. Mr. Corbin knew that Congress did not have to grant permission to Mr. Browne's plans. Daniel made a visit to the Northern Pacific Railroad Directors in 1886. The Directors agreed to work with him on the new railroad. During the next 20 years, Mr. Corbin built seven feeder railroads, which included a feeder in Spokane Falls.

The Union Station, built in 1914, was located on the north side of Trent

Downtown Spokane rail yards and train stations, circa late 1930s.
(Eastern Washington State Historical Society).

between Stevens and Washington. Work actually began in 1908 to lay track and construct the building. The building was more ornate and elegant than the Great Northern Depot. It was four stories tall, red brick and white stone, with terra cotta trim on the front. The inside area was grandiose, with immense chandeliers, high ceilings, and a wide staircase coming from the large entrance lobby below. On the north side of the building were the tracks, which were elevated, making it necessary for passengers to take another set of stairs to reach these trains.

The Milwaukee Railroad had a freight office located on the north side of Trent, two blocks west of Division. This building was a one-story structure. At one time, there were 14 loading docks on each side of the main building.

By 1924, the railroads had overrun Havermale Island and the south bank. On any given day in the 1920s, over 100 trains would roll through the city of Spokane. The trains loaded and unloaded twenty-four hours a day, and then made their way through the hills, fields, and some 500 little communities scattered in the region. With so many railroad companies in Spokane and with the majority of the lines either built by Jim Hill or merged to his lines, the city took on the name of the "Empire Builder."

By the 1950s, Spokane, was known as a railroad town, with tracks running throughout the downtown district. During this time, Spokane, as well as the entire nation, saw the decline of the passenger train service. People were beginning to travel by car due to better roads and more fuel efficient automobiles. As far as agriculture, lumber, and manufactured commodities were concerned the train system continued to be of paramount importance for business and jobs.

A Side Note.

Today, the clock tower of the Great Northern Depot stands alone at River Front Park. The building was demolished in 1973 to pave the way for EXPO 1974. Havermale Island is now a park where the Imax theater is located along with amusement rides, ice skating rink, miniature golf course and an outdoor concert arena. The island is a fun playground for the citizens of Spokane and its tourist.

A MEMORY OF DAD AND TRAINS

Dad and trains are linked together in my memories. I am not sure of the exact reason. Possibly, it was because Spokane was a city of trains when Daddy was growing up. Maybe it was his love for steam engines and old world technology. It could have been the romance and adventure that was once associated with trains, but my father loved anything that was connected to the world of trains. If we went to the annual Spokane County Fair, the first place my father would head to would be an area set up to view train cars and steam engines. On many a Saturday morning, it meant going shopping with him to hobby shops or train stores searching for the newest model trains sets. On other occasions, Dad diligently searched through the classified section of the ads in the Spokane Daily Chronicle or The Spokesman Review looking for trains sets that were for sale. Due to dad's love of model train sets, new friendships or acquaintances were made, and new trains purchased. It was always entertaining and exciting to see what new toy dad would bring home.

As a result of a number of years of Dad's searching, buying, selling and storing numerous model train sets, one corner of our basement, was designated as the area for Dad's abundant collection of model train sets. The many boxes went from floor to ceiling. His dream was to create a miniature display of various trains traveling through a metropolitan city, farmlands and near-by small towns.

Eventually, he achieved his dream. The dream cost money, took his time and challenged his handyman skills to build his display table. But in the end Dad constructed a 8-foot by 10-foot table that stood about three and a half feet high. There were numerous model trains following meandering rivers, passing trains while going through mountain tunnels, crossing bridges, and stopping in large towns and small farming communities. Daddy's dream took many years to complete, and at times, exasperated my mother, who didn't understand his passion.

Dad spent hours with his hobby. He amused us kids and our friends with his newly created villages and farms. We could spend hours watching the trains go round and round the many rows of railroad track that he laid. It took time to learn all the switching boxes and how they operated. Dad was most reluctant to let us kids operate the switching apparatus. Whenever our friends came over to play, Dad was always willing to show off his train exhibit.

A SIDE NOTE.

Of all the wonderful memories I have of my Dad, none are as strong as his love for his trains and of music. I can still remember hearing him belting out the old time favorite song by Patsy Cline, "Life is like a mountain railroad!" I can't remember all of the words but I know they included, "never falter, never fail. Keep your hand upon the throttle and your eye upon the rail!"

AN OLD MAN AND A BOY

I am not sure how it all began, and I am not sure if Richard knows. For whatever reason, there was an immediate bonding of friendship between my younger brother Richard and Eric. I have often thought Eric senior was possibly reliving the growing up years of his late son Eric junior. From the onset of their first meeting Richard became Eric's son, and grandson and constant companion.

Eric took Richard fishing, and taught him how to hunt. Eric purchased land near Sprague, Washington called the Pot Holes. On this land were small bodies of water surrounded by wild brush and grass. During the summer months, Eric would take Richard to the Pot Holes so they could build blinds for the fall duck hunting season.

Their time at the Pot Holes provided an excellent opportunity for them to work with the Labrador Retrievers that Eric bred and raised to show and sell. His hobby and passion were to teach these intelligent dogs how to be exceptional retrievers. Balls and fake birds would be thrown into the water holes. The dogs had to quickly run, dive, swim and retrieve the balls and fake birds for Eric and Richard.

Richard's birthday was the day after Christmas, and as a birthday present, Eric would take Richard to another place called the Pot Holes, which was a reservoir near Moses Lake, Washington. This would be another outing for hunting and working with the dogs.

During the summer months, Richard and Eric spent many hours painting decoy ducks to look like the real "McCoy." The purpose of these birds was

177

to assist the hunter by luring birds in flight to land on the water. Simply put, they were a trap. Eric also taught Richard the fine art of duck calling. On many a summer, day in our back yard or on the front porch, the two could be seen and heard practicing the various sounds that are needed to attract ducks. The two would spend hours hooting and whistling, hooting and whistling, and then hoot some more.

When they weren't busy preparing for the fall duck hunting season, they were busy talking about fishing, and where to go for the next fishing trip. These were usually weekend jaunts to Lake Pend Oreille in northern Idaho. As soon as school dismissed for summer vacation, Eric and Richard hightailed it out of town, and would head to Pend Oreille Lake for a week of solid fishing. Then, throughout the summer months, Eric and Richard would take some of Eric's closest friends to the majestic lake in northern Idaho for a day of fishing. Mom would bake cookies and make various kinds of sandwiches for them to take on their fishing trips. Most of their hunting excursions were very successful. Very rarely did they come home empty handed. On most occasions, they would come home with Idaho trout and steelhead. The best parts of these fishing excursions were the fish fries that took place at our house, and sometimes at the Aller's home. The aroma of fish frying and pies baking would filter throughout 22nd street. Tables and chairs would be set up in the back yard, and neighbors would bring a dish to share. It was a potluck extravagance. Mom always seemed to have an open door policy at our home. Everyone was always welcome to come and partake of a great meal and festive conversation. Sometimes, only a couple of families would come to the fish fries, and at other times, it seemed like everyone who lived on 22nd street was at our house, laughing, talking and consuming scrumptious amounts of delicious food.

At age 10, my brother learned how to drive a car, thanks to the talents and the insistence of Eric. Eric owned a long swept wing station wagon that he drove back and forth between the Pot Holes and Spokane. On several occasions when Richard and Eric were working at the Pot Holes preparing for the duck hunting season, Eric, for whatever reason, felt it would be a good idea for Richard to learn to drive. Why not? Farm boys learn how to drive tractors so they can help their parents on the farm during harvest time. To Eric, it just seemed logical that Richard should be able to learn to drive his big station wagon. Richard would come home from the Pot Holes and bound through the house with a grin on his face that would go from ear to ear. Eric took great pride in this accomplishment, but I am not so sure Mom and Dad felt the same way.

As days, weeks, months, and years slipped by their friendship grew. Our father was not interested in hunting and fishing, and felt honored that Eric took such a fond interest in Richard, and was willing to teach him the fine art of sportsmanship. Even though Grandpa Schafer was both a fisherman and a hunter, he seemed to have a group of old cronies that he enjoyed being with, and never took Richard or any of his grandsons along with him on these outdoor adventures.

As the years rolled by, Eric added Jim and Nicky Allers to these sporting events. This was a time for male bonding. The guys exuded a sense of pride and accomplishments when they walked through the front door with trophies of fish or fowl to feed the neighborhood.

PARTY TIME

Eric and Erna Bert loved to have parties and thrived on entertaining. Between the two they had a large circle of friends whose interest and backgrounds were varied and unique. When deciding to entertain, it did not make any difference if the party was for the adults or us kids. Reasons for entertaining were as wide ranging and diverse as their friends. Maybe they would choose to honor a friend's achievement, welcome a long-time friend to Spokane, commemorate a birthday, or celebrate an anniversary. Both were always looking for a reason to celebrate something. The couple worked hard and played hard. But playing meant including friends and families. Play time was their stress releaser from the grind of long hours and total commitment to the photography business. From the moment the Magney household moved to 22nd Street, Jack and Dorothy were always included in all of Eric's festivities.

Eric dearly loved children. He took great delight in helping children develop talents, win awards, set goals for themselves and then achieve that goal. He found that he could laugh at the simple things kids would say and do. It was also a way for Eric to heal the wounds he suffered when he lost his only son during World War II.

From the day that I first met Eric, we developed an immediate bond and love for one another that has always been difficult to explain. I was the little grand daughter he had been wishing for. Eric was to became my best friend, teacher, father, grandfather and superman rolled into one. Simply put, we adored one another. Eric was my hero and I was his little princess. He never missed a day to check on me, Richard, and Janice.

Every summer, shortly after school was recessed or summer vacation, Eric planned a special picnic in honor of the children he personally knew. Initially, the annual summer party for us kids took place at Eric and Erna Bert's home. As the years progressed, more of the picnics were held at Manito Park.

As I matured and grew a little older, Eric believed it would be good experience and good training for me to assist him with the planning of this exciting summer festivity. In planning for the van Werald annual kids' picnic, much discussion centered around, what would we eat, what games would we play, what kind of prizes we would buy, how many invitations should be purchased and who should be on the guest list.

Great concern was given when discussing the location. Eric preferred to have the kids' summer parties in his yard. Erna Bert however was never fond of this idea. She was a true artist and business professional. She did not have a passion for young children. As children grew and became young adults, she enjoyed their company. Basically, she felt younger children were a nuisance. Her concerns focused on the perceptions the public would have. She was fearful that always having a yard full of children would impact her photography business and customer relations in a negative manner. As the years passed, it became more evident that Erna Bert was not going to tolerate having fifty kids in her yard and running through the house to use the bathroom.

Eric always managed to rope Mom and Delores Allers into preparing some of the food for this festive event. Delores baked several desserts, and Mom made a couple of salads. They prepared enough food for fifty kids and ten adults.

The picnic was always a summer highlight. Two of my favorite memories were the Dixie cups that were filled with vanilla ice cream and orange sherbet. Eric made sure everyone received at least one. He stashed away several for himself, as this was one of his favorite desserts. The other favorite memory I have was being able to roast hot dogs and marshmallows on long sticks that Eric had personally made for the party. In early June, he would start collecting branches from the numerous trees that were in our vacant lot. He would spend time on our front porch or the back yard shaving the branches, until each one was long and thin, yet firm enough to hold the hot dogs over a hot flame. Eric had two methods for creating a fire to roast our hot dogs and marshmallows. Sometimes, he would dig a large circular hole in the ground. At other times, he would put briquettes in a wheel barrow, and we would roast our hot dogs in that fashion.

By the time I was 12, Eric was of the firm opinion and belief that it was significant for my proper upbringing to learn the fine art of formal adult entertaining. At least once a month, Eric and Erna Bert held a lavish dinner party in their home. Eric believed it was his grandfatherly duty and obligation to instruct me in the fine art of hosting parties. He began by instructing me on the proper way to set a formal table, including which lines to use, which crystal, sterling and china to select and where they were to be properly placed. Eventually, I was taught how to choose the correct center piece.

THE SPOKESMAN-REVIEW Sun., July 29, 1951. * * 3

Youngsters Entertained at Wiener, Marshmallow Roast

Mr. and Mrs. Eric Bax Van Werald entertained a number of neighborhood friends last week at a wiener and marshmallow roast in their yard at W234 Twenty-second. Seen toasting marshmallows over coals laid in the metal wheelbarrow are (front) Richard Magney and Howard Gabriel. Second row, Ricarda de la Fuente, Marilyn Magney, Monica Morton, Karen Goff, Fallon McDonald, Kathryn Morton, Donna May McDonald and Troni McDonald. (Erna Bert Nelson.)

The Spokesman-Review, July 29, 1951

The day the party occurred, Eric spent the entire morning moving out the cameras and the spotlights from the photography studio. Erna Bert knew in advance she could not schedule any photo shoots. Eric set up specially made round tables that would comfortably seat eight adults. What a chore it was to set thirty two places. Eric supervised my table setting progress by monitoring where I placed each piece of silverware and glass ware. If I made a mistake, he would come to me and rearrange the silverware or glasses. He never scolded me or raised his voice. He simply reemphasized the importance of having every thing in its proper place. I felt like I was his little princess, and he was allowing me the privilege to be part of his special party. As my table setting skills improved, I got to set the place cards in front of the dinner plates and put the elaborate centerpieces on the tables. I also had the honor of knowing what special recipe he was preparing for his guests. One of Eric's hobbies was cooking. He had numerous gourmet specialties that he enjoyed preparing.

Included at the van Werald celebrations were the Allers, Eugenes, Zilgmes, Aunt Ginny and Uncle Jesse, along with their numerous well known local artists and, at times New York and California celebrity friends.

BROKEN DISHES &
NO PASSPORT FOR MARILYN

When I was almost eleven years old, a monumental event occurred in my life. It is one of those major events which remains in a person's memory for a life time. No matter how old one becomes, the importance or the significance of the event never diminishes. One day Eric made an earth shaking announcement to Mom and Dad; he wanted to return to Holland and be reunited with member of his family. Now in his late sixties he decided he should begin the process of mending some broken fences (relationships) with his family. Eric had numerous discussions with Mom and Dad about the possibilities of me traveling with him and Erna Bert to Europe and Holland. There was, however, one big glitch to his plans; he wanted to remain abroad for six months or longer. According to Eric's plan, most of that time I would be with Eric and Erna Bert, and would have the educational opportunity of a life time, I would get to see most of Europe. For those occasions when I could not accompany them, I would be with a governess and private tutor. I would be well supervised and never alone.

After numerous discussions with me about the possibility of my accompanying Eric and Erna Bert to Europe, Mom and Dad finally consented to Eric's proposal. I was on cloud nine; an opportunity of a life time was at my feet. I was so excited! I was going to Holland and Europe. Eric quickly began making arrangements for me. He made long distance phone calls to his relatives, and asked them to begin an immediate search for a well-qualified tutor and governess. Plans had been set into motion, and the day finally arrived for me to get my passport. A few days later, Mom and Dad were ready to purchase my airline tickets. Just as we were getting ready to walk out the front door of our house, mom froze. "I can't do this," she said. "I can't let Marilyn go to a strange foreign country without me. She is only eleven years old. When she becomes ill, I won't be there to take care of her. Six months is too long for her to be away from her family. Eric and Erna Bert will have to go to Holland without her."

Mom called Eric and broke the news to him. He begged her to change her mind and promised that I would receive the very best of care. He tried to impress on Mom the wonderful education I would receive at such a young age. Mom would not bend. She would not change her mind.

Well, I did not go to Europe and neither did Eric. If I couldn't go, he wasn't going. He called off the entire trip. Erna Bert was livid with Eric, and furious with Mom that she had waited so long to make that crucial decision.

Erna Bert had a sharp tongue and was never bashful about using it. And use it on me, she did. She was angry with me because I stood in the way of Eric seeing his family and rebuilding some important relationships. She was upset that she was not going to have an opportunity to visit Holland and Europe. For the first time in my life, I was seeing a very jealous side to Erna Bert's personality. Resentment for me seemed to be oozing from every pore of her body, which greatly upset me.

Mom and Dad tried to console me by explaining that, because Erna Bert had never been a mother, it was often difficult for her to understand Eric's love for children. Mom felt badly that Erna Bert was taking so much anger out on me. Mom said she should have initially decided I could not make the trip. Dad's explanation was, Eric had adopted us as his new family, and in the process of doing so, we had become the priority in his life. In essence, we had become his life line, his joy and his future for his aging years. When his son was killed during the war, Eric's world crumbled around him. Gone was the joy and the laughter. That all changed when we moved into our new home on 22nd Street. Now in his senior years of life, he was not about to be away from his new family. It was pure and simple; if I couldn't go, he wasn't going.

He placed numerous phone calls to some very unhappy family members in Holland. To soften the blows, the disappointments and the hurts, Eric promised to bring some of his family to America the following summer. Within a few months of those phone calls, Eric received the sad news that his brother had passed away. Learning this news bothered me for a while. I felt that I had cheated Eric out of seeing his brother for the last time.

Eric kept his word and the following summer, his widowed sister-in-law came to America. I was most apprehensive about meeting his Dutch sister-in-law. I was fearful she might be angry with me. Instead, she embraced me with hugs and kisses, and presented me with a gift. Today I still have this gift, and bring it out only during the holidays of for special celebrations. It is a sterling silver Dutch spoon with a picture engraved in the spoon.

Erna Bert never did seem to forgive me for disrupting their plans to see Europe and visit family in Holland. To add fuel to the fire one summer, when I was thirteen years old, Eric decided to have an extravagant dinner party. He invited fifty plus guests to this special affair. Usually, he limited the number of quest to thirty two. As always, I was in charge of setting up the tables. For this occasion, however, he believed I would need some extra help to prepare for the party. He asked one of my best friends, Arlene Allers, to help me wash the dishes as the guests were finishing their meal. This meant we had to act the part of waitstaff and dishwasher.

To this day, I believe that Arlene and I made a good team. We understood our responsibilities and understood the importance of clearing the tables in an orderly fashion. We also knew the importance of getting the silverware and crystal goblets to the kitchen sink pronto.

Eric with his over generous heart had invited too many people to the party. He was under the assumption that some of his guests would cancel or send their regrets. No such luck. Anyone who received an invitation to one of the van Werald parties knew they were in for a gastromic gourmet treat, and very rarely declined such an invitation. Now we were faced with the problem that there was not going to be enough silverware and crystal goblets for everyone. Eric soon realized he had to change his dining strategy. His new plan would be to serve the food buffet style, and guests could choose to sit wherever they felt comfortable.

Arlene and I managed to monitor the activity in both the upstairs and the downstairs. We quickly removed dishes that were dirty, washed them and immediately place them back on to the buffet table. The two of us were a great team. Our mothers and Eric, had trained us well. The assignment was working-out to be a piece of cake. We were out to please and provide quality service. And service with a smile we did provide. The majority of the evening progressed extremely well for us. But towards the end of the evening, as Arlene and I were trying to hurry through the last round of crystal goblets, one of us tripped on the throw rug in the kitchen and bumped into the other, who was carrying a tray of the glassware. All of a sudden, there was a loud shrieking crash and screams produced by both Arlene and me. There on the kitchen counter and the kitchen floor lay broken tiny bits and pieces of the very finest cut crystal from Denmark. We had just destroyed a dozen water goblets and wine glasses that had been in Erna Bert's family for many generations.

Beside Eric racing up the stairs, our parents came rushing to our rescue. Nothing can compare to the horror I saw on Erna Bert's face when she saw her fine crystal smashed to smithereens. Erna Bert wanted Arlene and me to immediately leave her house. We were full of apologies. It was an accident. Nothing had been broken intentionally. Eric felt very bad, and said that he would clean up the mess. Our fathers, however, had the broken class cleaned-up within minutes. That was the last time Arlene and I washed dishes at Eric and Erna Berts. Not only had I ruined Erna Bert's trip to Holland and Europe, but now I had broken her beautiful crystal goblets that were a family heirloom.

SEVERAL SIDE NOTES.

As the years passed, Erna Bert eventually learned to forgive me. For many years, however, she did not want to be around me. I was the sore spot in her life. It wasn't until I was married and with children of my own that she truly relinquished the anger she had towards me. Time has a marvelous way of healing our hurts and disappointments. Erna Bert learned to love and to forgive, and a unique bond formed between the two of us. When we would get together, we would reminisce about that monumental moment in our lives.

As the years passed, she looked forward to the times when I would bring my children to her home, so she could visit with them and take their pictures. On one occasion, my three year old son, David, became very excited when he learned he was going to be making a visit Erna Bert's house. He thought we were going to be going to Ernie and Bert's house. When I shared this story with Erna Bert, she laughed hysterically and went to the book store and bought David a special Sesame Street book that had a picture of Ernie and Bert on the cover.

Sadly, my children never had an opportunity to know Eric. Eric died very suddenly and unexpectedly, when I was seventeen. When Eric passed away, Erna Bert assumed his role of grandparent, friend and mentor. She graciously accepted her new position in the Magney family. Not only did she grow to love us but as the years quickly slipped by and her own health was failing she seemed to treasure our company.

One of Eric's most loved dinners was his Wild Duck Feast. He took great delight in preparing the duck he had shot while hunting at his Pot Holes.

Many folks do not care for wild duck. But devouring one of Eric's ducks was a gastromic delight. His birds were succulent and flavorful. He placed the fowl in a large roasting pan with salt and pepper. Next, each bird received a full cube of butter. He then covered the birds with a generous amount of red wine. When the ducks were almost cooked, he would add heavy cream and mushrooms. This meal was never intended to be served to anyone who was on a diet or watching their weight.

SCHOOL DAYS

I have some good memories, and some not so good memories, of my early educational experience. My generation was part of the baby boom that began at the end of World War II with the return of the GIs to public life.

The public school system in Spokane, and throughout the country, was not adequately prepared to deal with the onset of hundreds of new little tykes in the public school system. Districts were scrambling to find qualified teachers, hire strong principals and locate resources to construct new buildings to house the onslaught of new students. This scenario was very true for School District 81.

In 1951, when I started kindergarten at Roosevelt Elementary School, there were several one story portable buildings throughout the campus. These separate units were used as classrooms, because there was inadequate space in the main building. The old school was a two story brick structure that housed a lower level for the gymnasium and restrooms. The second floor held classrooms for the upper grades and the school library.

From kindergarten through sixth grade, there was a minimum of thirty students in my class. Discipline was strict. Students avoided being sent to the principal's office. Girls were not allowed to wear pants to school, not even in the cold winter months. Chewing gum was outlawed by teachers, the principal and possibly the PTA! The County Health Department sent nurses to the public schools to assist the school nurse with inoculating students for polio, mumps, small pox and providing physical exams for scoliosis.

I can't remember the name of my kindergarten teacher, but I will always have fond memories of the grade school I attended. Roosevelt School was named after Theodore Roosevelt and the original Roosevelt School was housed in a four room frame building built in 1906 and located at S. 1415 Bernard.

In 1907, a new brick building containing eight classrooms was built at 14th and Bernard. In 1910, five classrooms were added on the rear of the building.

The first class of eight students graduated from the eighth grade in 1912.

Cub Scout Pack 4 started at Roosevelt in 1916 and still carries on the tradition of scouting, as Pack 304 is at Roosevelt today.

1917 saw the addition of the eastern wing of the building. In 1925-1926, grades 4 through 8 were set up on the "platoon system." Students moved from teacher to teacher after a homeroom period. For art classes, students met on a daily basis with art teachers.

The school structure remained the same until the 1954 addition of the brick multipurpose unit on the south side of the school was built. Frame construction was added to the east of the brick building in 1955 and 1958 to provide six additional classrooms

The "Cafeteria" program began in 1925 when the school principal, Miss Witt, started an annual affair for the children who liked to bring their lunches to school or have a picnic. In 1940, when Miss Witt retired, a new principal took over the reigns and suggested that it might be a great money raiser for the school if the relatives and friends of the children and members of the PTA came to the "Cafeteria." Eventually the "Cafeteria Day" became known as the "Gala Day."

Mr. Everett Henderson was the school principal when I started kingergarten. He, along with mothers who were very involved with the schools activities, initiated a special event lunch program, where children paid twenty five cents and adults paid fifty cents for a meal. Mothers who belonged to the PTA association prepared the food. They would bring hot dishes, sandwiches, jello and cakes to the school. Proceeds from the annual affair were for children's needs at the school.

Mom participated in the lunch program in a couple of ways. She prepared large quantities of food, and phoned other parents, signing them up to bring various dishes to the school. Other PTA moms volunteered to set out plates and silverware or participate on the clean up committee.

Another fun event' occurred late in the spring. This was the annual spring carnival, which was sponsored by the PTA. The carnival took place on a Friday evening and many fathers assisted with this fund raiser. Mom baked a number of cakes for my favorite game, the cake walk. Dad volunteered to sell tickets. Both Mom and Dad assisted with the clean-up.

A variety of student presentations were a part of almost every PTA meeting. Fifth grade students reported on geography, history and the culture of Russia, followed by a short play and dances. Poems, recitations, singing, tumbling demonstrations, band and orchestra presentations were all included. Demos of new equipment were also held. During the fifties, the PTA Safety Committee made continual attempts to get traffic lights installed at 14th and Lincoln, and 14th and Grand for the safety of students walking to and from school. The PTA began work to improve the playground.

Roosevelt could boast it had a good size gymnasium that included a very large stage. Both were used by the public for plays and various civic events. This space was especially beneficial during the holiday season. The school produced an elaborate Christmas play which was attended by people in the neighborhood, as well as the families of students.

Students in all grades were asked to try-out for the production. This was a time of year when the students could share their talents with parents, grandparents and the entire student body.

Each grade level formed a choir, and the music teacher chose songs that were appropriate for each grade. The best part of the Christmas pageant was the moment we would relive the birth of Christ. When I was in the second or third grade, I was selected along with six other students to be one of the angels. I was elated, but it meant Mother had to create an angel costume for me. She was not a seamstress and hardly knew how to operate a sewing machine. Our good friend and favorite babysitter, Clara Hickman, came to the rescue. Clara had an artistic flare with her sewing and asked Mom for either thin wire or thin clothes hangers. She planned to make my angel wings with wire, white bed sheets and gold tinsel.

Thanks to Clara's designer skills and great sewing abilities, I ended up being the best looking angle in the Christmas pageant. My costume was long and flowing with wings that extend high and wide and glittered as the spot lights shone on me. I was in seventh heaven and relished in all the attention.

On October 18, 1954, 263 students were served the first hot lunch in the new cafeteria. The PTA bought the tables for the new addition. I loved taking hot lunch during the winter months, even though it meant standing in a long line and waiting my turn. Each classroom had to line up along the wall and, of course, the youngest classes were served first. Lunches were full of starchy mashed potatoes, macaroni and cheese and great desserts like chocolate cake.

Teachers and the school principals strongly encouraged all students to be involved in school activities. Students would receive awards by participating in such things as the Scholastic Art Exhibit, a school hobby show, or a family fun night. Boys from Roosevelt, in the mid fifties, made up a dance band called the Starlighters.

The principal whom I remember the most during my school years was Mr. Arthur B. Dunning, who came to Roosevelt in 1956. During that time, the student body enrollment continued to climb. When I began the seventh grade in 1958, there were 676 students in the school.

My eighth grade class was the last eighth grade class to graduate from Roosevelt. School District 81 had just completed the construction of a new school building that would embrace a new concept. September 1960 would see seventh and eighth grade students attending Sacajawea Junior High School near Grand and 36th. The student population at Roosevelt dropped to 466 students.

Teachers make a huge impact on the lives of their students. My favorite teacher at Roosevelt was my third grade teacher, Mrs. Coon. She taught us how to write stories by looking at the covers of POST or LIFE magazines, which usually displayed the latest Norman Rockwell drawing or painting. She believed each piece of art work created a story. Our class assignment was to write a story based on what the picture was saying to each of us.

I learned the most from my sixth and seventh grade teachers, Mrs. Cromwell and Mr. Wickstrom. Mrs. Cromwell loved the theater and poetry, and assisted with all school plays. She made sure her students were involved with all things related to drama. She also had a great love for geography and history, and placed a positive emphasis on learning about people from other countries.

Mr. Wickstrom was the strictest teacher I had ever experienced, a no-nonsense man who had been in the military for a number of years. He tolerated no back talking, demanded perfection and never accepted an excuse if assignments were half completed or turned in late. He did, however, motivate his students to learn and have respect for one another. He was hardest on the boys in class. Today I am thankful for Mr. Wickstrom, and believe schools should have more teachers like him.

School was never easy for me. I assumed it was because my mother did not allow me to use pencils and crayons nor did she work with me on arts and craft projects when I was four, five and six. Listening to music and reading stories was important to her and her goal was to encourage my interest in theses areas.

During a kindergarten conference, I still remember the teacher telling Mom I was academically behind the other students in my class. My teacher recommended spending more time working with me on my hand co-ordination, learning my numbers and the alphabet. She gave Mom a variety of ditto sheets consisting of coloring in the lines, and numbers and letters to trace with a pencil or a crayon. My muscle, hand and eye co-ordination were more like that of a typical four year old.

In addition, my attention span was not up to par, and the teacher pointed out that I could be intimidated easily. I was, however, polite and a joy to have in the class room. The teacher believed it was to my advantage to walk to school with other students, and was glad to know that Mom had made such arrangements. It's hard, now, to believe that I could remember this from kindergarten days, but it apparently made a lasting impression on me as I listened to this parent-teacher conference. Perhaps it was the beginning of my belief that I was dumb and could not learn.

My fourth grade year at Roosevelt was a real struggle for me. For whatever reasons, my mind shut down and I stopped learning. Mom and Dad were most concerned about my attitude for they could see I was struggling and falling behind. During the summer months, Mom and Dad were debating if they should hold me back and have me repeat the fourth grade, whether they should send me to a private school, and if so, which one, or should they hire a special tutor for me. Summer passed quickly, and no decision was reached. I began my fifth grade year at Roosevelt.

Uncle Jesse and Auntie Ginny who lived a few blocks south of us on 26th were concerned about cousin Karen, and decided to remove her from the public school system. From some Christian friends, they had learned about a new private elementary Christian school which was beginning its second year. The school had acquired an excellent academic reputation for its high school. The Junior High and the Elementary School had not been in existence long enough to establish a reputation for excellence in academic standards.

The biggest disadvantage to us was the location of this new Northwest Christian school, for it was on the far north side of Spokane. It was so far north, it was at the end of the Cable Ad bus line. The good news was that bus transportation on the public transit system was available. At the beginning of the school year, Aunt Ginny and Uncle Jesse visited the school and enrolled Karen. During Karen's first week, they visited again to be certain they had made the right choice for their child.

I began my fifth grade year hating school and trying to find reasons not to attend. Mom and Dad were very frustrated with me. At the insistence of Aunt Ginny, Mom decided to call the private Christian school and set up a visit with the principal.

Within a week, I was enrolled and spent my fifth grade year at Northwest Christian School. To this very day, I know God was guiding my parents to make this crucial choice for me, although I did not know it then. This change had a life altering effect on rest of my life. I will be eternally greatful to God and my parents for that monumental decision.

The history of Northwest Christian School began on a cold, blustery

March evening in 1949 when a group of very active evangelicals representing the local chapter of the national Association of Evangelicals, gathered together to pray and discuss their vision of a future Christian high school. This group of pastors worked hard to develop inter-denominational ministries such as the Inland Empire Sunday School Association, and the Inland Empire School of the Bible. Rev. Sherman A. Williams, pastor of Beacon chapel, Rev. Dr. Walter Bridge, from First Baptist Church, Rev. Alvin Delamarta, Queen Anne Free Methodist church, The Rev.Everett Backlin, Broadway Baptist Church, Rev. Clate A. Risley of Hillyard Baptist Church, Rev. John B. MacDonald, Knox Presbyterian Church, and Rev. E.C. Deibler, of Fourth Presbyterian Church were just a few who participated in this event.

In all, over 40 churches were represented at that meeting, and thus Northwest Christian high School was conceived. A Board of Regents was established, along with a Board of Education. Those serving on the Board of Education from 1949 to 1951 were E.J. Fadel, Principal: Everett Armstrong. Chairman: Dr. Walter Bridge, J.M. Yaryan, E.D. Orcutt, Rev. Sherman A. Williams Jr., and Stanley Mallery. These board members met weekly during the summer months planning the building phases and the opening for the new high school in September, 1949. J. Wright Baylor was the Superintendent, and Bruce Mc Cullough, chairman.

Ground breaking for the Christian high school was June 26, 1949. Twenty eight acres of land was purchased for $7,000 in the N.W. section of Spokane at the corner of Central and Cedar where a campus was to be developed. Buildings that housed the administration and the class rooms were given by the government (Farragut buildings, worth $200,000.) In addition to the buildings, God provided lots of low cost labor, volunteer help, gifts from building supply firms, and other donations.

A conservative estimate of the value of the land and the developments in 1950 was estimated at $350,000.

The city Planning Commission gave their official approval for the school plans. On July 11, 1949, Northwest Christian became incorporated.

By August of that year, four teachers were hired, and 62 students had registered for school.

Fourth Presbyterian Church (now Fourth Memorial) was the first site of the new Christian high school. The Church Board voted to invite the school to use the church facilities free of charge, and on September 7, 1949, Northwest Christian School opened its doors for the first time to excited students and parents.

School hours were from 8:50 am to 3:30 pm. Tuition was $10 a month for 9 school months, making it one of the lowest tuitions in the nation. Out-of-town students were offered room and board at Christian homes for reasonable rates, or a chance to work in exchange for room and board.

School Superintendent, J. Wright Baylor said, "This church is especially suited to our school needs. It is close to two bus lines, Hillyard and Wellesley; it has sufficient classroom space, has hot lunch facilities and has a gymnasium. It is only a few blocks from Mission park so we can make use of tennis facilities there."

The first year of the school was difficult and, like all new beginnings, experienced many new birth pains. When school started at the Fourth Presbyterian, it was very crowded even with the small enrollment. Classrooms were too small and the space inadequate. The Board decide the school had to move.

The First Assembly of God was building a new church and graciously invited the school to move into the second floor of their education department. The building was unfinished, but the nice large classrooms were greatly appreciated by the students and teachers. Before the end of the year, however, the church needed to finish the education department for its own use, and Northwest Christian High School had to move again.

On March 30, 1950, the third location for the school was the old Hillyard Baptist Church, where the school completed its first year. The resolve was to be in the new school located at the corner of Central and Cedar Streets by September 1950.

In May 1950, Northwest Christian High School graduated six seniors and ended the school year with 72 students. Those first graduates were Gene Morehouse, Harold Winters, Vearl Greenwood, Marjorie Unruh, Betty Zinn and Phyllis Unruh.

The first year was extremely difficult. Finances presented many obstacles to the new school. On several occasions, there was not enough income to pay the staff their salaries. Many thought that the school would not be able to open for the second year. Only $2,000 of the $30,000 needed had been raised by September 1950, but after hard work, many sacrifices, lots of prayer and faith, the school opened in the fall of 1950, but still at the Hillyard Baptist Church.

The Board of Regents, and The Board of Education set goals for the school to move and add buildings from the Farragut naval station. During the summer following the conclusion of the first year, enough buildings were hauled to the campus to enable the school to move into its new home during the spring of the second school year, March, 1951.

During the next few years, wonderful things would transpire for the school. New desks were purchased in 1951. The school published its first annual in 1952, and three years later, hosted the Northwest Fellowship Christian Schools Musicale. The final performance of the musical was held at the new Spokane Coliseum on Boone.

While many hurdles had been jumped, God was placing a new burden on the hearts of the Board members and the school's Christian leaders. By 1953, there were twenty parents who had indicated their desire to have their children attend a Christian elementary school.

There was room at the high school, but it would take considerable remodeling. It was estimated that an amount of $5,000 would be needed to ready four large rooms for grade school in the fall.

On May 24, 1953, Northwest Christian announced in the Spokesman Review that the school would be expanding and starting a Christian elementary school. It would begin in the fall at the old Madison grade school at Dalke and Division. Mr. Fadel, the Principal, reported that the high school had 100 students enrolled for 1953, and he estimated that would increase by 40 students for fall enrollment.

By 1954, Northwest Christian added the Jr High, and the following year, in 1955, added the Elementary School with bus service on the north side of town.

For whatever reason, I was excited when Mom and Dad shared with me the news that they had reached a difficult decision. They were going to be pulling me out of Roosevelt Grade School, and I would be attending the same Christian School as Karen. I was elated!

This news, I was to learn, was not so well received by Karen. We both had much to learn and many new adventures to experience. There would be a very long, drawn-out bus ride clear across town. As fall and winter months approached, I could be seen standing on the corner of 22nd and Bernard waiting for the Cable Ad bus to pick me up at 7:30 each morning. Come rain, snow, ice or high winds, there I was along with several adults who were catching the bus to get to work. The good news regarding the transportation nightmare was that I would not have to transfer buses. It did make for a long ride and an even longer day, for this ten year old.

The first few months, my fifth grade class shared a room with the junior high students. Poor Karen! She was so-o-o-o blessed to have a tag along cousin sharing the same teacher and the same room. This set up did not last long, however. About six weeks into the year, a new teacher had been hired, and an additional room was set up for the junior high students. I remained in the same room with the sixth grade and the fourth grade students. My teacher for my fifth grade was Mrs. Hoff.

God truly worked a marvelous miracle in my life by bringing this wonderful teacher and devoted Christian lady into my life. Everything that I failed to learn in the fourth grade, plus what I needed to know for fifth grade and sixth grade, I learned in one year.

Our typical class day began with prayer and Bible reading. Can you believe that when I learned to really read and read well, the book Mrs. Hoff had me read was none other than God's word. What an amazing concept! I doubt that concept would be used today, or perhaps not even thought of, by most teachers. But I thrived and blossomed every time I picked up a Bible.

God was working a miracle in my life. Hallelujah! This reminds me of an old hymn, "Revive Us Again." The chorus to that hymn is "Hallelujah! Thine the glory, Hallelujah! A-men: Hallelujah! Thine the glory, revive us again!" I was beginning to feel revived and alive. I was not the dumb bunny I thought I was!

In addition to providing me with a reassuring and understanding teacher, God supplied me with new Christian friends. One of those dear friends was Lois Mc Roberts. Lois was my age and looked something like Shirley Temple. She had the longest and the thickest ringlets I have ever seen. It wasn't until she was a teenager that she was able to say goodbye to her curls. She was an only child whose parents had married rather late in life. They were shocked when they learned their family was growing to three, but Lois was full of energy and bubbled with enthusiasm for life. She could sing and play the piano, but of more importance to her parents, she was being raised and taught in a surrounding of Christian teachings and principles.

The McRoberts were devoted Christians who attended River of Life Church between Wellesley and Francis.

Lois and I enjoyed taking turns staying over night at each other's home. On one occasion when I was staying at their home, we attended an evening church service. It was at this church service that Mrs. McRoberts extended an invitation to me to accept Jesus as my Lord and Savior. That evening, in the small little Assembly of God Church, I gave my life to Christ. First God

ONT ROW: Gregory Block, Mike Tinn, y Ellen Palmen, Kris Johnson, John mas, John Palmen, David Hamilton, n Stern, Laura Moore, Dana Kennedy. SECOND ROW: Jean mas, Lois McRoberts, Stephen Buick, Harold Thomas, Clyde m, Douglas Anderson, Ricky Simmons, Kurt Johnson, Linda lin, Janis Doolin. THIRD ROW: Miss Sue Woelk, Jim Cobbett, a Martin, Kenneth Enquist, Lynne Anderson, Marilyn Magney, Cobbett, Billy Goerz, Richard Ceaser, Mrs. Hazel Hoff. Pictured: Walter Palmen.

GRADES

MR. & MRS. E. A. HAYDON

helped me to grow intellectually, and now he was helping me to grow spiritually. Praise His Name!

By the time I finished the fifth grade at Northwest Christian, Mom and Dad felt I had made wonderful advancement, academically and emotionally. They wanted to see if I could survive in the public school system. I was very disappointed when I learned I would be going back to Roosevelt School for my sixth grade. I had made wonderful friends at Northwest Christian and I did not want to transfer! I was able to progress with some degree of confidence, due to the wonderful support I had received from Mrs. Hoff. She prepared me for the sixth grade challenges by teaching me to always trust in God, and when needing help, call on the name of Jesus. In my eyes, she will always be my Number One teacher.

After I returned to Roosevelt Elementary School, I found I wasn't as dumb as I had believed I was. Former school friends were glad to see me. Mrs. Cromwell was an outstanding teacher, and helped me to grow and expand my horizons. I learned the fun of sports such as volleyball, girl's basket ball and softball, thanks to help from Mrs. Mauro.

Today, Roosevelt Elementary School is not the same as I remember. The old building is gone, and in its place is a new modern structure that houses grades K-6. Teachers whom I knew, have of course, retired. The same is true for Northwest Christian School, which has grown and expanded. The High

FRESHMAN CLASS

FRONT ROW: Marion Hoff, Beverly Palmen, Kay Shrock, Karen Scholl, Barbara Hammond, Andrea Lunde. SECOND ROW: Roger Hartman, Leslie Martin, Colleen Caldwell, Sally Williams, Karen Groff, Gary Herning. Not Pictured: Patricia Day.

JUNIOR HIGH

School and Junior High School are no longer at the Central Campus. In May 1996, the Board of Regents purchased 116 acre site in Colbert, WA., 10 miles north of the Division Y. This site was previously known as the Bishop Tope Center. Included in the 42,000 square foot buildings are a large chapel, classrooms, practice gym, dining facilities and sports court. Plans were made to retrofit the buildings. In 1996, the new high school opened in the fall to excited students and teachers.

TO GOD BE THE GLORY FOR GREAT THINGS HE HAS DONE!

June 16, 2000, Northwest Christian celebrated 50 years of providing Christian education, glorifying God by pursuing academic excellence within a Bible-centered environment.

To all of the teachers who have helped me struggle with the learning process, I salute you. It was not until I became a mother, and had a child who also struggled with reading, writing and math, that I fully understood what the term 'dyslexia' means.

A SIDE NOTE:

A wonderful part of my education was attending weekly Bible School Classes at St. John's Cathedral. St. John's Cathedral is located on Grand Boulevard and 12th. The location was the site for the home of Francis Cook who is considered to be the Father of Manito Park. The Cathedral was built in 1927. For more than seventy-seven years, this magnificent structure has been a historical land- mark in Spokane.

The church was more than seven blocks from Roosevelt Grade School, but our classes were dismissed once a week for one hour, so we could be taught the word of God. The Church volunteered its space, and parents volunteered their time walking us kids to and from the school and the church. Another set of parents prepared in-depth Bible lessons and taught them to an audience of 50 or more children at one time. We always opened with prayer and sang a few songs, and then we heard the stories from the Old and New Testament.

My favorite teacher at Bible School was Mrs. Donald Harvey, who was a very active member at First Presbyterian Church. Betty Harvey was the wife of dentist Donald Harvey. She loved to teach, and especially loved to talk about Jesus. God blessed this special lady with a marvelous gift, and she willingly shared it with many children. She came prepared with wonderful flannel board cut outs, and I can still remember looking forward to hearing her tell a Bible story.

At age seven or eight, my heart grieved the day I learned there would be no more Bible School. The church was willing to share the space, the parents were more than willing to volunteer their time, and Betty Harvey never did stop talking to children about the love of Jesus Christ.

The school was closed for a number of reasons. One of the reasons was due to a women named, Madelyn Murray O'Hare. A devoted atheist, she was opposed to praying in public schools, wanted total separation of church and state, and was opposed to schools using government funding to teach the word of God. The issue produced lots of debate and many heated arguments. Because the school district was receiving state and federal funds, the district made a decision to no longer permit its students to take an hour off during the day for Bible Study classes. What a heart wrenching day for this young miss when I could no longer go to the beautiful cathedral with its stained glass windows, and listen to Betty Harvey tell of God's promises. How sad that

Front of Northwest Christian Elementary School. Even though this picture was taken in 2003, the school looked very much the same in 1956

future generations were denied this special treat. It was here that God was laying a foundation for my soul. It was in that Cathedral I learned to sing "Go Tell It On the Mountain," "I have Decided To Follow Jesus," and "Peace Like a River."

Today, parents still love their children, and still participate in school life. While many may not be as involved in daily school activities as was the norm in my day, parents still want to be a part of that segment of their children's lives.

I will always believe that what has been called the O'Hare decision was one of the saddest points for the fifties and for education in the public school system. I believe many of the problems we have encountered in the years that followed resulted from this ending of Christian teaching.

W. 333 - 14th Avenue Spokane, WA
Constructed in 1906 the original school was named for Theodore Roosevelt,
who was the current president of the United States.
Photo courtesy of Eastern Washington State Historical Society.

REFLECTIONS

Looking back on the years I spent growing-up in Spokane, on 22nd Street, in the fifties; I have come to realize the uniqueness of this city and its people. I will treasure the little neighborhood on 22nd Street, which was tucked away from the hustle and bustle of buses and cars and crowds of people. I have come to appreciate that our lives were built on a strong Christian foundation, where permanent roots could grow and flourish. Parents raised their children believing there would always be a better tomorrow, a bright future and a pot of gold at the end of the rainbow. Friends and neighbors were never intimidated by the thoughts of tackling new problems, or seeking help and advice from one another, no matter how complex the issues.

Writing this book has rekindled old memories and rediscovered that old friendships never die, but only grow stronger with time.

Spokane, 22nd Street and the Fifties is dedicated to honor God, family and friends. It celebrates the strong ties and bonds that existed between groups of people. The book is a celebration of the lives of those folks, the strong bonds of friendship and the commitment they all had to one another. The commitment was unspoken and unwritten. It was the commitment of love and acceptance that was continually at work while God was watching over us all.

A FINAL SIDE NOTE:

As I finish the last chapter I want to pay a tribute to the men and women who left a positive influence on my life while growing up in the fifties.

All of the men but two have passed away.

At eighty five, Jesse Groff and Aunt Ginny are still living in their condo. Irene and Edmunds Zilgme and Delores Allers remain in their homes on 22nd Street.

My two grandfathers taught me that there is no such thing as retirement. Grandpa Magney passed away when he was one hundred years old, and stopped working when he was ninety. Grandpa Schafer decided to retire from URM when he was eighty one years old. Howard Allers never stopped building his beautiful grandfather clocks. Uncle Jim worked in his law practice until he was in his eighties. Bob Nix was an active volunteer at First Presbyterian Church for many years.

The women who nurtured me through adolescence and into the adult years of my life, never stopped baking goodies, painting pictures, sewing clothes, fluffing pillows for overnight guests, visiting the sick in the hospital, or praying for others. I guess the women of Spokane and 22nd Street never had a chance to retire or think about growing old. They were too busy making the world a better place for everyone, and most of all, ME!